GW00771632

Anglicans
on
High

A selection of Suffolk churches and
Suffolk people who have been part of
the Catholic Revival in the Church of England

© The Fitzwalter Press and Taverner Publications, 2014

ISBN 1 901470 21 0

British Library Cataloguing in Publication Data

All rights reserved.
No part of this publication may be reproduced, stored in a retrieval system, or transmitted,
in any form or by any means, electronic, mechanical, photocopying, recording or otherwise,
without the prior written permission of the Publishers.

Printed and sponsored by POSTPRINT
Snetterton Business Park, Snetterton, Norfolk NR16 2JZ

Contents

To the Reader

Bibliography

Chapter One

The Catholic Movement in the Church of England

Chapter Two

Some Suffolk Churches and Clergy

Chapter Three

Brief notes on other Suffolk churches associated with the Movement and some of their clergy

Chapter Four

Some Notable Clergy

Chapter Five

Religious Communities

Chapter Six

Opposition and Persecution

Appendix

Colour Photographs – Ancient & Modern!

To the Reader

IT WOULD TAKE a mighty and lengthy tome to do proper justice to the full extent of the Catholic Revival's influence upon the parishes of Suffolk, because so many of them have been touched by it to a greater or lesser extent at different times and every parish church in England, its life and worship, has been influenced by it.

What follows is just a small miscellany of churches, parishes, people and events that I have gleaned from a variety of sources over a number of years. There are many gaps and I know that there are more churches and people that could have been included. Conversely, I am aware that some readers will think that my scope has been far too wide and that maybe only those churches and people described by me as 'advanced' or 'extreme' really qualify. I realise also that my terminology might cause purists to cringe, because I have tended to use words which have been coined as jargon either by the movement or by its opponents. Usually however, I have done my best to place them in quotes! The variety of terms used to indicate the Holy Eucharist are usually quoted from the relevant parish document, so may appear as a 'Celebration', 'Holy Communion', *Missa Cantata*', 'Sung Mass', 'High Celebration', etc. Where dates appear beside a priest's name they usually refer to his time in the parish rather than his birth and death.

Most developments over the past 25 or so years are conspicuous by their absence and this little survey deals mainly with the first 150 years from the Assize Sermon in 1833. I have deliberately stopped before the vote in Synod to allow the ordination of women to the priesthood, the aftermath of which has had a tremendous effect upon Anglo-Catholics and other Anglicans.

Despite these omissions, I hope that what follows may provide something of interest to today's Anglicans of all traditions and indeed to all Christians, whoever or whatever they are. Bearing in mind that the Catholic Revival has left its mark upon the churches, parishes and people of Suffolk, I hope that this book may inspire interest and curiosity in historians, church-crawlers and all who love and study our county.

This second edition of *Anglicans on High* would not have been possible without the assistance and skill of Gudrun and Jeremy Warren and the staff of Postprint.

Roy Tricker, January 2014

Sources used and Select Bibliography

A Short History of the Oxford Movement — S. L. Ollard
Life & Personal Reminiscences of Samuel Garratt — Evelyn R. Garratt
Romanism and the English Church — Reproduced from *The Record*
Corpus Domini and Other Poems — The Rev'd Sandys Wason
Twenty Years at St Hilary — The Rev'd Bernard Walke
Something Beyond — A. F. Webling
The Call of the Cloister — P. F. Anson
St Alban the Martyr, Holborn — G. W. F. Russell
Why I am an Anglo-Catholic — G. A. Cobbold
John Kensit, Reformer and Martyr — J. C. Wilcox
Father Burn of Middlesbrough — T. G. Fullerton
Quam Dilecta — W. A. Whitworth
Building up the Waste Places — P. F. Anson
The Enthusiast — Arthur Calder Marshall
The Akenham Burial Case — Ronald Fletcher
All Hallows, Ditchingham — Sister Violet, CAH
Mr Wason, I Think? — Roy Tricker

The Clergy List.
Crockford's Clerical Directory.
Kelly's Directories of Suffolk.
The Ritualistic Clergy List.
Minutes of Evidence of the Royal Commission on Ecclesiastical Discipline.

Numerous histories and guides to Suffolk parishes and churches.
Parish Magazines and Church Periodicals.
Documents relating to parishes, now deposited in the Suffolk Record Office.

Church services registers, mostly deposited in the Suffolk Record Office.
Our beautiful churches themselves, and their contents, which have been my major source.

Chapter One

The Catholic Movement in the Church of England

LOOKING AT THE CHURCH OF ENGLAND TODAY, we see a grand and glorious comprehensive school, whose wide arms embrace a multi-coloured spectrum of Christian thought and tradition, and accommodate a kaleidoscope of forms of worship and witness. It enables schools of Christian individuals to grow and develop spiritually, nurtured by the Anglican diet of Holy Scripture and the tradition of the Church, seasoned by God-given reason and enquiry.

Basically, the major traditions of the Church of England fall into three groups, although there is variety within each group, which would claim to have its "liberals" and its "conservatives". There are the Evangelicals (sometimes called "Low Churchmen"), who place their emphasis upon the sole basis of the Bible, preaching the Gospel of personal salvation by faith in Jesus Christ. There are the Broad Churchmen, who embrace a multitude of traditions, usually taking a "middle of the road" position with regard to worship. One might include (with tongue in cheek), when trying to think up labels for some of the Broad Church traditions, groups like "The Non Party Party", "The Non Extremists Either Way", "The Liberal Theology Party", "The Church of England by Law Established Party", "The Civic Church Party", "The Plain and Simple Country Religion Party" or even the "Tory Party at Prayer". Only the Church of England could ever get away with a mixed bag such as this – but it appears to work well because of its variety and there is room for just about everybody within its care.

The third group are the Anglo-Catholics (sometimes, although not always accurately, termed "High Churchmen"). The Anglo-Catholic does indeed have a "high" regard for the Church; he sees the Church of England as the Catholic Church of this country and (together with the Roman Catholics and the Eastern Orthodox Churches) part of ancient traditional Catholic Christendom. He sees the Church of England not as a Protestant sect invented at the Reformation, but as the same English Church which reached our shores in the 2nd or 3rd century, was spread by the early Celtic missionaries, was brought more into line with Western Christendom at the Synod of Whitby in 664, was made even more continental under the Normans, was enriched during the Middle Ages by glorious architecture, churches, liturgies and ceremonial, and was reformed during the 16th century; a church whose threefold ministry of Bishops, Priests and Deacons hold valid orders through the Apostolic Succession and effectively minister the seven Sacraments of Baptism, Holy Communion, Confirmation,

Matrimony, Penance *or* Reconciliation, Holy Orders and Holy Unction. Amongst the many things that Anglo-Catholics see as being important, the following may be regarded as paramount:

1. The importance of the Church, its teaching, tradition and interpretation of the Scriptures; also the position of the Anglican Church as part of Catholic Christendom and its relations with its sister Churches.

2. The importance of the Priesthood and the Sacraments as fundamental in the life of the Church.

3. The importance of the Holy Eucharist as the Church's central act of worship, where Christ becomes specially present as the Church perpetuates and proclaims His sacrifice on the cross.

4. The importance of the Sacrament of Penance and the authority of the Church to declare God's forgiveness of sins.

5. The importance of order, dignity, colour, majesty and symbolism in worship, according to ancient (but ever-changing) tradition and enriched by the use of lights, vestments, incense, the sign of the cross, genuflexions, bowing, etc., to glorify God.

6. The importance of discipline in the Christian life, in careful preparation and attendance at worship, in the use of Offices, the Sacraments, forms of Devotion, etc.

7. The importance of devotion to the Mother of Our Lord and to the Saints, also caring for our departed loved ones by praying for them.

In today's Church, the Anglo-Catholic is not the only person to have a high regard for many of these things and for the many other things which are held to be important, but it has not always been so and to see why we must go back over 200 years.

The Sleeping Church and its Evangelical Awakening

AFTER THE STRUGGLES of the Reformation in the 1500s and the turmoils of the Puritan take-over during the mid 1600s, with their bloodshed, battles and strife, the 18th-century Church settled down to a comparatively peaceful existence. After the Restoration of the Monarchy in 1660 its position as the State Church, by Law Established, was secure and its status in English society was highly regarded, with the result that spiritually it gradually drifted off to sleep! The ungodly alliance between Church and State meant that the former became little more than the handmaid of the latter. It has been described as a glorified branch of the Civil Service, which was expected simply to back up whichever political party held sway! Many of the clergy were members of the land-owning families and hundreds more were spiritually ignorant. Several of the bishops (who often reached their positions through nepotism or political affiliation) spent little time in their dioceses and hosts of clergy were non-resident, employing poor and often uneducated curates to rush from parish to parish in order to "read divine service". The scandal of simony abounded, whereby clergy secured responsible positions by offering money to patrons and the disgrace of pluralities was all too frequent, with clergy holding several parishes, often miles apart, and drawing their income whilst rarely visiting them.

Sunday services often took place in dirty and poorly maintained churches, where congregations sat, according to their social classes, in commodious box-pews, with the Squire and his family often aloof in the chancel, all listening to (or ignoring!) their bewigged parson reading a social or moral treatise. Holy Communion was an appendage to the service, which took place about four times per year. It was not unknown for the church font to end up as an ornamental flowerpot in the Squire's garden! Many baptisms took place in private houses, although as late as 1840 men and women flocked to Plymouth Church on "Christening Sunday" to act as sponsors – the fee for their services being a pint of beer!

Many examples can be quoted of the misuse of churches and their furnishings, wrong-doing and laziness amongst the clergy and general neglect of real Christianity during this period, although it must be remembered that there were many faithful and industrious clergy who did their best for their people and tried hard to care for them and to nourish them spiritually. The general picture, however, particularly at the top of the ecclesiastical hierarchy, was one of neglect and gloom. Two great revivals, so very different from each other, were to pull the Church of England out of the depths and to awaken some spirituality into her. These were the Evangelical Revival and the Catholic Revival, both of which were to shape the two great traditions in the Church of England today.

The Evangelical Revival began during the 18th century with a few Anglican clergy and lay-folk who saw the need for real personal Christianity, which was so sadly lacking in the Church. They preached the Gospel simply and sincerely and led people to a personal faith in, and relationship with, the living Christ. Sometimes this happened through a definite conversion, where a person became aware of his sin and the need for a saviour and as a result he repented and turned to Christ. The Evangelicals bombarded the Church with plain and forthright Bible preaching, the fight against sin and Satan in society and in people's souls. Their zeal and sincerity filled their churches and brought many to a personal faith in the crucified Saviour. The names of John Wesley (who to his dying day remained an Anglican) and George Whitefield stand out in this revival, but it gradually gathered momentum in many Anglican parishes in the late 18th and early 19th centuries where notable preachers packed their churches and influenced other clergy also. The fiery Parson Grimshaw of Haworth, who left his congregation before the sermon to walk to the local pub to compel its occupants to come to the church with him and hear the Gospel, pulled down his church because it was too small and built a new one. On his Sacrament Sundays as many as 1,000 communicants could be expected. Amongst other notable parish clergy were Henry Venn of Huddersfield, John Venn of Clapham, John Fletcher of Madeley and Hugh Stowell of Manchester. Daniel Wilson of Islington transformed his sleeping parish so that when he left it was covered by house-to-house visitors, fifteen Sunday Schools functioned and three new churches had been built. At his first Confirmation he presented 780 candidates to the Bishop. Perhaps the best known of all was Charles Simeon of Holy Trinity, Cambridge. He founded the Simeon's Trustees, who acquired the patronage of livings all over the country, so that clergy could be appointed to those parishes who would maintain Evangelical principles and preaching. He acquired St Peter's, Ipswich in 1801 and appointed the talented Evangelical preacher, the Rev'd Edward Griffin, who remained until 1833. Under his leadership St Peter's was the first of several Ipswich churches to come under the influence of the Evangelical Movement. Griffin founded one of the first Anglican Sunday Schools here and the church was packed on Sundays to hear his preaching. Members of St Peter's became known in the area as "Griffinites".

By the 1830s the initial blast of the Evangelical Revival was winding down – not that it had failed, but it was beginning to become an established tradition within the Church, and one which was to grow, develop, change, evolve, and maybe occasionally to act unwisely, but certainly to be an effective force of the Holy Spirit to influence the Church for untold good, as it does to this day. The Evangelicals made a great impact in many places; they were particularly predominant in seaside resorts and in fashionable places like Bath, Cheltenham and Tunbridge Wells, yet in so many towns and villages the old "Low Church" party prevailed – a very different set-up. These were the "old guard" – liberal and wishy-washy theologically, dependent upon the pandering to the State, and generally spiritually dormant. The hunting, shooting, fishing and Squirecreeping parson was still regarded by many people as the "norm" and the Evangelicals as being rather excitable and odd.

The Oxford Movement and the first stages of the Catholic Revival in the Church of England

THE CATHOLIC REVIVAL was born in the University of Oxford. Those who gave birth to it were mostly Oxford dons and were brilliant scholars. During its early years its ideals were spread by preaching and writing and only very gradually were any changes seen in the churches of England. This Oxford Movement followed in the wake of the Evangelical Revival and it awakened the Church to other vital things, which for years had lain dormant. Since the Reformation there had always been "High Churchmen" who stressed that the Church of England was part of the Catholic Church, hence holding a "high" ideal of its authority, and emphasising the importance of its Priesthood and its sacraments. The Movement was launched in 1833 and caused a tremendous explosion which was to have a dynamic effect on the Church of England, changing and enriching it and leaving its mark forever upon it. The spark which ignited the explosion occurred when Parliament in its wisdom decided to cut the number of Bishops in Ireland by ten. This interference by the State in Church matters brought forth a fiery sermon (the Assize Sermon) on 14 July 1833 by the Rev'd John Keble, in Oxford's University Church of St Mary the Virgin.

Suffolk was involved at the very beginning of the Movement because, as a result of the Assize Sermon, a four-day Conference was held ten days later in the library of the Deanery Tower at Hadleigh – the residence of Hugh James Rose, who was Hadleigh's parish priest from 1830 to 1833. Rose had expressed views which were in line with the Oxford Movement seven years before it began. He was a distinguished Cambridge Scholar and Chaplain to the Archbishop of Canterbury. He preached at Cambridge in 1826 a course of sermons on the Christian ministry which firmly reasserted Catholic teaching. In 1832 he founded the *British Magazine* as a journal for disseminating "sound" church views. He built the present parsonage house in Hadleigh beside the Deanery Tower, he improved the school and founded a parochial library, he introduced the practice of catechising the children for an hour before the morning service: he worked hard at Hadleigh despite his rather delicate health. In September 1833, Hadleigh hosted a huge confirmation for the surrounding parishes and 195 of the candidates were Hadleigh parishioners. Rose left Hadleigh to become Professor of Divinity at Durham University and was later Principal of King's College, London. He died in 1838 at the early age of 43.

Three other eminent scholars took part in the Hadleigh Conference. These were William Palmer, an Anglican Divine whose scholarship was respected and treated seriously by Roman Catholics and who had good and close relations with many important clergy; Arthur Perceval, Rector of East Horsley, Surrey and Chaplain to the King; and Richard Hurrell Froude, Fellow and Tutor of Oriel College, Oxford, poet and scholar, former pupil of Keble and close friend of Keble and J. H. Newman – a sincere and disciplined High Churchman, who was horrified at the state of the Church of his day.

It was hoped that the conference would establish an association in defence of the Church and its principles, but this did not happen. Instead it was decided to send an address to the Archbishop of Canterbury, urging support when the Church had to fight for the Apostolic Succession and 230,000 heads of families signed the accompanying address. The Hadleigh Conference was enough to make churchmen aware that people were beginning to campaign for a right understanding of the Church. The Assize Sermon and the Conference provided a starting off point for the Movement. The Hadleigh delegates were described as "slow and respectable men" who wanted to go carefully and therefore hopefully to carry the Church dignitaries with them, with the possible exception of Froude – and it was he and his friends at Oriel College, Oxford who took the Movement from there by more direct and potent agitation with the issuing of the *Tracts for the Times.*

Among the major figures who emerged as leaders of the Movement were three Fellows of Oriel. These were: John Henry Newman (1801-90) who was Vicar of the University Church and who became less active in the Movement in the years preceding his secession to the Roman Catholic Church in 1845; Edward Bouverie Pusey (1800-82), Professor of Hebrew and Canon of Christ Church, Oxford, who was the acknowledged leader of the Movement from 1845; and John Keble (1792-1866), Professor of Poetry and, from 1836, Vicar of Hursley, Hampshire, who had preached the Assize Sermon in 1833.

Steered by these and other brilliant scholars, the Movement began to spread its teachings through a series of volatile little *Tracts for the Times* (hence the term "Tractarian"), which were dispersed to rectories and episcopal palaces throughout the country and caused much ferment and interest amongst bishops and clergy. The final tract (Tract 90), written by Newman in 1841 about the 39 Articles, intending to show that the Church of England had by no means discarded its Catholic nature when it broke with the Church of Rome, caused such a storm that the series was brought to an end. More trouble then came when some of the Movement's activists despaired so much of the attacks made by Liberals, Evangelicals and the church hierarchy that they felt that the work was becoming a lost cause and so made their submissions to Rome. These included J. H. Newman and H. E. Manning, both of whom later became Cardinals.

One Suffolk priest who was associated with these early years of the Movement was the Rev'd Samuel Rickards, who had also been a Fellow of Oriel College and knew the founders of the Movement well. He was a particularly close friend of Newman, with whom he was in regular correspondence. Newman often stayed at his vicarage at Ulcombe, Kent and later at Stowlangtoft, near Ixworth where he was Rector from 1832 to 1864. He wrote to Newman upon his arrival in Suffolk that the people there were 'either of the lowest order of Dissenters, or else they were Churchmen without a jot of Christian knowledge'! Although a keen supporter of the Oxford Movement, he never became extreme or advanced in his churchmanship. He hated any idea of a movement towards Rome and when Newman left the Church of England in 1845 all communication between the two friends ceased. He did, however, have his beautiful church tastefully restored in 1855/6 to the designs of William White, the eminent Gothic Revival architect who also designed some Anglo-Catholic churches in London and elsewhere.

Out of Oxford and into the Parishes of England

AS TIME WENT ON the Movement grew and developed, extending beyond the cloistered courts of Oxford and into the parishes, where ordinary English folk came under its influence, and where its principles were to develop along various channels during the rest of the 19th century. As a result, church buildings were restored on mediæval lines, with raised altars, often furnished with crosses and candlesticks, because churches were being regarded less as preaching-houses and more as places where heaven and earth meet in the Holy Eucharist. In an increasing number of English churches the Holy Communion was celebrated weekly, and sometimes daily, with proper observance of Holy Days and Saints Days in the Church Kalendar. Many clergy were saying their Offices daily and in a disciplined manner; they were also caring for their peoples' spiritual and physical well being.

The whole basis of the early Tractarians' work was to answer the question, 'What is the Church?' and so to bring home to people that it was not a mere branch of the Civil Service, but was no less than the mystical Body of Christ on earth, living His life and under His authority, governed spiritually and pastorally by worthy bishops and clergy in the Apostolic successions, who were concerned not only with preaching and "reading the service", but also in nourishing folk with the Sacraments of the Church. As a result, theological colleges for the training of the clergy were set up, schools, orphanages and hospitals were founded and run by the Church, attempts were made to revive the monastic life and people were being taught and encouraged to pray. Their parish church not only demanded their loyalty, service and care, but also in return cared for them and provided them with spiritual nourishment.

As the Movement spread and particularly as several churches were developing their worship and ceremonial along rather extreme lines, opposition grew from the old Low Churchmen and also from the Evangelicals with whom the Anglo-Catholics had so many fundamental points in common, although their approach was often different. Those who clung to the old State Church religion felt very threatened by the Movement and did all in their power to stop its spread. Evangelicals protested with greater thought and misgiving, particularly as those who became known as Ritualists were pushing the limits of Anglo-Catholic worship further and further towards what Evangelicals saw as unadulterated Popery.

In 1865, the Church Association was established to 'counteract the efforts now being made to pervert the teaching of the Church of England on essential points of Christian Faith and assimilate her services to those of the Church of Rome'. Known by its opponents at the "Church Ass", this body brought many ritual cases before the courts in the hope that litigation would stamp out the Catholic Revival.

In line with the teaching about the Church, the priesthood and the sacraments, the expression of Catholic worship was accompanied by ceremonial and, because this seemed to be the natural development of pre-Reformation ceremonial, it usually followed that many of the practices in use in Roman Catholic churches were incorporated into English Catholic worship; clergy who used these were known as Ritualists. Where the average parish church was having Morning Prayer, with the priest in surplice, often changing into his black gown for the sermon (a practice regarded as "Sound" by the Evangelicals) the Ritualists were celebrating High Mass, with surpliced choirs, lighted candles, eastward-facing position at the altar, processions, water mixed with wine in the chalice, eucharistic vestments, incense, etc. – all of which were loathed as Popery by the Evangelicals – in churches adorned with statues, sanctuary lamps, Lady Chapels and, as time developed, with the Blessed Sacrament reserved in a tabernacle behind the altar or an aumbry in the wall.

People were being taught about the Real Presence of Christ in the Bread and Wine and the Mass as the Christian Sacrifice. They were being encouraged to make their confessions, to love and venerate the Mother of Our Lord, to pray for their departed loved ones and to ask the saints to pray for them. The Evangelicals saw all this as a sell-out to the Church of Rome and the Church Authorities saw these developments as being totally strange, definitely illegal and having no place in the Church of England. Bishops refused to consecrate churches because there was a cross on the altar or an illegal side chapel and enraged Protestants interrupted services and bribed gangs of local yobs to cause riots, disturbances and brawls.

Dean Close once stated that 'The restoration of churches is the restoration of Popery' and it is true that not only restoring churches, but also the building of many new churches which sprang up in the second half of the 19th century, was a product of the Oxford Movement, although many Evangelical churches were beautifully restored and several fine new ones were built. Some Evangelical clergy were careful to make sure that their churches were refurbished in such a way that it would be impossible for a successor to institute ritualistic practices in the building without spending a great deal of money on further alterations. Conversely, new Anglo-Catholic churches were sometimes built with the minimum of decoration so that no objection could be raised at the consecration, but with plenty of scope for future generations to add things to make the interior beautiful and devotional.

Clearly the authorities had to act if the Ritualists were to be put down, so in 1867 the Ritual Commission was created to look into the differences in ceremonial practices in the Church of England. Reports were produced about vestments, lights and incense, etc. which were looked down upon by most of the Commission's members. This hurt the Anglo-Catholics when attempts were made to enforce the Commission's findings, and when forbidden practices were not abandoned the Public Worship Regulation Act came into being. This Act of 1874 was intended to suppress the growth of ritualism once and for all. Offenders were reported and could be summoned to appear in court before Lord Penzance (an ex-divorce court Judge) and they were ordered to comply with its findings. Those who refused could be deprived of their livings and otherwise punished in some way. When the court dared to go as far as imprisoning some of the priests who refused to comply with its orders – perhaps most notably Fr Arthur Tooth, parish priest of St James, Hatcham in south London – many reasonable folk felt that this was going too far and that irreparable damage was being done to the Act.

There were, however, plenty of Protestants who were keen to spy on the ritualistic churches and to make the fullest reports of the illegal practices that they had managed to sniff out. Towards the close of the century, John Kensit and his followers, who were determined to put down ritualism, began to make their impassioned stand against it, causing friction and disturbance wherever they went. Mr Kensit and his descendants led the Protestant Truth Society, which still functions. He and his followers hunted out many offending churches and exposed the "evils" which took place in them, sometimes securing successful legislation against them. Their dramatic "exposures" of frightful goings-on did the Anglo-Catholic movement untold good by creating tremendous interest in it, also much sympathy for it from ordinary English folk who abhorred rudeness by people who deliberately created disturbances or irreverently interrupted the worship of others. Many anti-ritualistic books were produced, including Walter Walsh's great tome *The Secret History of the Oxford Movement* which inadvertently made Anglo-Catholicism seem so exciting and challenging that it has been the unwitting cause of several conversions to the Movement!

The scraps and persecutions of the ritualists make fascinating, if sometimes sad reading, but they did not crush the Movement – rather they made it thrive. Many of its churches were full, its people committed and devout, and this was largely due to the faithful priests who worked themselves to death (sometimes literally) for their people. There were so many dedicated and saintly clergy, particularly those who came to work in slum parishes without hope or wish for preferment or fat stipends. Their lives were disciplined, their love and care for their people earned the devotion of their parishioners and even admiration from fair-minded folk from other traditions within the Church. Their fine churches, richly furnished and constantly prayed in, together with their beautiful services, brought ordinary people close to Jesus and provided majesty, mystery and beauty for the poor folk, whose lives were often very mundane and bereft of colour.

As the 20th century progressed, much of the active persecution of Anglo-Catholics lessened, although there were many instances where bishops refused to visit "extreme" churches to administer confirmation or to license curates to serve in their parishes. There were also occasional court cases – mostly arranged by the Protestant Truth Society – resulting in illegal furnishings being removed from churches by order and even acts of wanton vandalism by opponents of the Movement. All they needed to do in an offending parish was to find one aggrieved parishioner whom they could persuade to complain, and then they could try for litigation. The Church of England had embraced many things that the early Tractarians had fought for and their work had been vindicated. Even the more extreme Anglo-Catholics, if not always approved of by the Establishment, were tolerated and left alone. Also the Church at large began to realise and recognise the hard work done by Anglo-Catholic clergy and also what a tremendous amount these people had to offer the Church at large. An increasing number, therefore, were made honorary canons, were elected to Convocation and the Church Assembly, and a few even became bishops.

Anglo-Catholicism at its most triumphant expressed itself in the great Anglo-Catholic Congresses held in London and in various provincial centres in the 1920s and 1930s, where the faithful from all over the United Kingdom demonstrated their solidarity and gathered in their thousands to hear great preachers and to attend High Mass in the Royal Albert Hall, the great London centres of the Faith or in huge open air settings like the White City Stadium or Stamford Bridge Football Ground. Here they could share in grand processions, glittering and triumphant ceremonial, worship embellished with rich vestments, clouds of incense and glorious singing. What was more, however, they could celebrate unashamedly the fact that the deep truths which these trimmings heralded had been restored to the English Church and that those who suffered persecution to secure all this for the church had triumphed and their cause had been vindicated. The congresses culminated in the Fifth Anglo-Catholic Congress which celebrated the centenary of the Oxford Movement in 1933.

Many priests and people expressed their solidarity with the Movement and also deepened their own spiritual lives as well as enjoying fellowship and fraternity with their fellow Catholics by joining themselves, or affiliating their parishes, to the various Catholic societies, which had mostly grown up during the latter part of the 19th century. These societies have also played an important part in spreading Catholic teaching and establishing it in the parishes. The Society of the Holy Cross was founded in 1855 for priests to 'maintain and extend the Catholic Faith and discipline and to form a special bond and union between Catholic clergy'. The Church Union (formerly the English Church Union) was founded in 1859 to 'recall the Church of England to her Catholic identity' and has always been one of the best known and recognised Catholic Societies. The Confraternity of the Blessed Sacrament was founded in 1862 to encourage devotion to Our Lord in the Sacrament of the Eucharist. Others include the Guild of Servants of the Sanctuary, founded in 1898 for servers at the altar, the Catholic League, founded in 1913 to foster union with the See of Rome and to spread the Catholic Faith, and the Society of Mary, founded in 1931 to promote devotion to the Mother of Our Lord.

The Guild of All Souls, founded in 1873 to encourage prayers for the departed and to care for the dying and bereaved, also procured the patronage of several livings and thereby has maintained the Catholic tradition in many of these places, although the grouping together of country parishes has hindered this somewhat during recent years. Similarly the Society for the Maintenance of the Faith (founded in 1871) also administers the patronage of livings all over England.

The revival, in 1922, of pilgrimages to the Shrine of Our Lady of Walsingham has provided a further and very important focus of devotion for Anglo-Catholics and particularly for people living in Suffolk, who have only to travel to the neighbouring county to visit the Shrine.

The almost single-handed revival of the Shrine by Fr Alfred Hope Patten, Walsingham's remarkable and dynamic parish priest, was a product of the Papalist movement within Anglo-Catholicism. Anglican Papalists were influential in the Catholic Movement between c.1900 and 1960 and their influence continues, especially through the Catholic League. They were considered by many Anglicans to be very "extreme" because their goal has always been corporate reunion with the Holy See. Many Papalists regarded the Church of England as a limb of the great Western Church which was brutally severed at the Reformation and is therefore in schism. So they were "in" the Church of England, but not "of" it, accepting without question the infallibility of the Pope and embracing all Roman Catholic dogma, belief and practice in faith and morals, using the Roman Missal and Kalendar (sometimes also the Latin tongue) and often furnishing their churches to rival the most *outré* continental shrines. They also encouraged dialogue with the Roman Catholic Church, in which Fr Donald Rea of Eye played an important part. St Mary at the Elms, Ipswich and Kettlebaston have had Papalist parish priests and Fr Philip Gray of Mendlesham has been Priest-Director of the Catholic League.

A great influence on the development of 20th-century Anglican worship (and one which was detested by the Papalists) was the movement for Parish Communion, which had its roots in Anglo-Catholicism and was promoted by the Parish and People Movement between c.1949 and 1970. Amongst other things, Parish and People strove to make the Parish Communion the central act of Sunday worship in parish churches, rather than Matins or the non-communicating High Mass. A few pioneering parishes had introduced this in the early years of the century and Parish and People did much to change the character of Sunday worship in churches of many shades of churchmanship. For Anglo-Catholics their work was vindicated when the Second Vatican Council ordered that the Parish Mass, with Holy Communion, in the language of the people and of the day, should be the central act of Sunday worship for Roman Catholics.

Some trends in Catholic worship

As WITH THE OTHER traditions within the Church of England, the Catholic tradition has expressed itself in different ways and by different degrees. There is the liberal element and the more extreme element - the Papalist element and the more profoundly Anglican element. There are, therefore, Catholic parishes which follow more closely the Prayer Book tradition and those who follow more closely the Roman Rite. Some are very traditional, even today, whilst others have branched out into the charismatic and other movements. Some people's Catholicism is seen more in their mode of worship whilst others express it more in their missionary interest, social concern or spiritual development. Within all these – in true Anglican fashion – there are a host of permutations also!

There have been – and there are still – many clergy who would call themselves and their parishes Anglo-Catholic, whilst their churches would appear to some to be very "middle-of-the-road", although the priest is a devout Prayer Book Catholic, carefully teaching his people to value the Eucharist, the sacraments, the saints, etc, but within the context of the *Book of Common Prayer* or, more likely nowadays, *Common Worship* and without many of the "trimmings". He may not even wear vestments or have a weekly Sung Mass, or even reserve the Sacrament. He will probably tell you that the early Tractarians did not do these things either, but he will also tell you that he is one with them in their vision of the essentials of the Faith.

Several parishes still express Catholic worship in the old English, or Sarum tradition (known by those who dislike it as "British Museum Religion"), which aims to return to the ethos of English worship during the Middle Ages – the worship for which our mediæval churches were built. Their clergy carefully follow the recommendations of the Rev'd Percy Dearmer, whose vast knowledge of the minutiæ of Sarum worship may be read in his manual *The Parson's Handbook*. They will treasure the heritage of the English prayer books, especially the First Prayer Book of King Edward VI, also many of the pre-Reformation customs, liturgical colours, styles of vestments, etc. This tradition encourages long, flowing surplices, albs and amices with beautiful apparels, altars framed upon three sides with curtains, hung between four riddel posts, possibly surmounted by gilded angels bearing candles, with usually two candles upon the altar itself (although some churches find room for six, as in the Western tradition). The Sacrament is reserved in an aumbry, or occasionally in a hanging pyx above the altar. The Church's year is often punctuated by occasions like Rogation processions, Plough Sunday, feasts of Dedication and of Title of the parish church, etc. The tradition was gloriously brought to life at Thaxted, Essex by Fr Conrad Noel – and what better setting for it than this gem of an English parish church in its glorious mediæval market town – where bell ringing, folk music, Morris dancing, craft guilds and a host of customs from Merrie England were all incorporated into the life and worship of the Church. Not a biretta was to be seen, nor lace cotta, Roman Missal or fiddle-back chasuble, but the worship was moving and magnificent. Many churches with a central tradition have used the Sarum style when equipping their sanctuaries – and very beautiful these are. The designs of F. E. Howard and H. Randoll Blacking in the 1920s, 1930s and 1940s, also the influence of the Warham Guild craftsmen, who made and promoted English vestments and furnishings, have greatly beautified our churches. The following illustrations taken from *Directorium Anglicanum,* a book published less than thirty years after the Assize Sermon kindled the flame of the Catholic Revival, perfectly illustrate the Sarum tradition.

+ Priest in Surplice Hood & Stole + | + Acolyte or Lay Clerk + | + Priest vested in Cope +

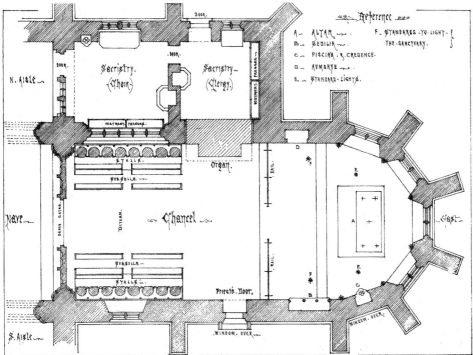

Chancel &c.

General View of Chancel Arrangements

✠ Altar &c ✠ Oblation of the Elements ✠ Book and Desk

It is, however, the churches of the Western tradition that most people would easily identify as being "real Anglo-Catholic". The thinking behind this tradition is that Catholic Christendom did not stand still, nor "freeze" at the Reformation, but has developed since, and over the past 400 years church furnishings, customs and worship have evolved – so we must look to what the Western Church (expressed in the Roman Catholic Church) has done and must model our worship upon this. As a result, Western churches became furnished as richly (or sometimes more richly) than contemporary Roman Catholic churches, even to the extent of using pseudo-Baroque and continental styles in the design of altars, reredoses, statues and other fittings. In these churches we would expect to find six tall candles on the shelf (or gradine) behind the High Altar, a tabernacle for the Reservation of the Sacrament, statues of Our Lady, the Saints, the Sacred Heart, etc. and maybe even a Confessional box. In the more extreme churches the Roman Rite may be used for the Mass rather than the rites based upon the *Book of Common Prayer* although nowadays many churches of this tradition find the options in *Common Worship* perfectly acceptable. We would expect to see the choir and servers wearing cottas rather than surplices or albs; also plenty of lace embellishing cottas, altar hangings, etc. Clergy would appear in close-fitting soutane cassocks and birettas, rather than the Sarum loose fitting double-breasted cassock and square Canterbury cap. The Roman Catholic services and customs of Benediction, the Rosary, processions of the Blessed Sacrament, etc., would be part of church life, although the Sarum advocates would regard these as modern Roman innovations.

Before the 1960s we would expect to see the Mass celebrated daily in Anglo-Catholic churches, and that the main Sunday morning (never evening) Mass would be billed as Sung Eucharist, or Sung, Solemn, or High Mass. The people were not generally expected to communicate at this service – they should have received Holy Communion, having duly fasted, at the earlier Low Mass. At this service one would expect to see the use of lighted candles, Eucharistic vestments, use of the Sanctus Bell, wafer bread, and mixed chalice (a little water ceremonially added to the wine) and the priest using the eastward position at the altar. In many "advanced" churches, the service might begin with the Asperges, using Holy Water, the priest might say the prayers surrounding the Consecration "in secret" (inaudibly and maybe even in Latin) and the service might end with the saying or singing of the Angelus and the reading of the first 14 verses of St John's Gospel. In certain churches with fine choirs the musical setting to the Mass might be a complicated one, maybe by Mozart or Palestrina, rendered by the choir and occasionally accompanied by an orchestra.

The Second Vatican Council (1962-65) not only brought about radical changes in the Roman Catholic Church and its worship, but also affected Anglo-Catholics, who felt that they should follow the lead given by the Western Church. As a result the westward position at the altar has been adopted in most churches, also the bringing of the main altar nearer to the people. It has also become the practice for everybody to make their Communion at the main Sunday Parish Mass, and Anglo-Catholics began to have Masses in the evening (something which they had always frowned upon). The Anglican experimental services and their culmination in the *Alternative Service Book* (1980) and *Common Worship* (2000) has brought services in most Anglo-Catholic churches more into line with the other Anglican traditions, because the essentials that they needed and used in the Mass have been catered for in the new Anglican rites. It might therefore be more accurate to say that so many of the things that the earlier Anglo-Catholics fought for have been accepted by many Anglicans and that the new liturgies have brought the Church more into line with them! In fact, the Catholic Revival has had a lasting effect upon the Church in so many ways, not least in introducing into common Anglican usage so many things which people of most Anglican persuasions accept as normal today.

Some fruits of the Catholic Revival in Anglican church life today

SEVERAL CUSTOMS which many Anglicans regard as normal today in churches and services were illegal a century or more ago and those who dared to use them were opposed and even punished for their efforts. Today clergy and people of the majority of Anglican churches, including many Evangelicals and some who would be quick to criticise Anglo-Catholicism, are now enjoying many of the privileges for which they fought.

The following, for example, were declared to be illegal at various times during the second half of the 19th century by ecclesiastical courts:

- Credence tables
- Altar candles when not needed to give light
- Standard candles in the sanctuary
- Paschal candles
- Embroidery or lace on fair linen cloths on the altar
- Coloured altar frontals
- Crucifixes
- Banners
- 'Images of the Baby Jesus' at Christmas
- Stone altars
- Reredoses
- Second or third altars (in side chapels)
- Crosses on, attached to, or behind the altar
- Flower vases on the altar
- Gates to the chancel
- Not displaying the Commandments on the east wall
- Eucharistic vestments
- Stoles (at Weddings, Baptisms or Holy Communion)
- Copes in parish churches
- Mitres
- Robed choirs
- Preaching in surplice rather than gown
- Embroidered crosses for decoration (even on bookmarks for the lectern Bible)
- Using the Sign of the Cross (especially by the priest when pronouncing the Blessing)
- The eastward position at the Altar

- Use of wafer (unleavened) bread
- Mixing water with the wine in the chalice
- Performing the ablutions after Holy Communion in the church during the service
- Reservation of the Sacrament for any purpose
- Processions as special parts of services

Needless to say, the following were most certainly out of order:

- Confessions
- Prayers for the departed
- Holy Water
- Incense
- Stations of the Cross
- Statues of the Virgin Mary or of the Saints.

Looking at other facets of the Church of England, her worship and practice, it is interesting to see how many are the direct or indirect results of the Catholic Revival. The following are but a few examples:

- The careful training of the clergy at theological colleges
- The emergence of the Holy Communion as the central act of worship
- Holy Communion weekly rather than quarterly
- Holy Communion on Saints Days and other weekdays
- Robed choirs seated in the chancel
- The use of servers, processional crosses, banners, etc.
- The popularity of Patronal Festivals, Midnight Communion at Christmas, special Holy Week services, Rogation processions, the distribution of palms on Palm Sunday, Harvest Festivals
- The use of Compline and other ancient Offices
- Retreats and Quiet Days
- The presence of monks, friars and nuns in the Church of England
- Even the Week of Prayer for Christian Unity has its roots in the Movement.

Chapter Two

Some Suffolk Churches and Clergy

WE HAVE the Catholic Revival to thank for the fact that the majority of our churches stand as they do today. Churches and church restorations of the 19th and 20th centuries may not be to everybody's taste, but thanks to the timely intervention of the Victorian restorers, responding to the need to make our churches safe, clean, beautiful and conducive to worship, many churches were saved from ultimate ruin and were adorned with beautiful ornaments and fittings. Several new churches were built in Suffolk as the population increased, or because their mediæval predecessors were beyond repair.

During the 18th and early 19th centuries, many church buildings were neglected and shamefully treated and attempts at restoration were often very cheap patchings-up, usually in brick. The fashion in architecture was predominantly Classical, inspired by ancient Greece and Rome, or rather debased forms of Gothic. The church was seen more as a preaching auditorium, usually filled with commodious box-pews (which were owned or rented by parishioners who could afford them), gathered around the large three-decker pulpit, which often stood about one-third of the way down the nave, westwards from the chancel arch. The chancel was also cluttered with these boxes, where people sat with their backs to the altar, which was often little more than a rickety old table which people had been known to use as a resting place for their hats or belongings, or even for church cleaning utensils! At Felixstowe in the mid 19th century, Lady Login only managed to stop the practice of the choir-men nonchalently tossing their hats into the font upon entering the church by half-filling it with water one Sunday!

In 1839, John Mason Neale and Benjamin Webb founded the Cambridge Camden Society to promote the study of ecclesiastical architecture. The more progressive members of this group formed themselves into the Ecclesiological Society in 1845. The Ecclesiologists not only fostered interest in the preservation and restoration of churches, but also tried to educate people in the "correct" methods of church design and furnishing. They advocated restoration and the building of new churches along pre-Reformation lines and principles and therefore revolutionised church building in the 19th century. They insisted that Gothic was the true Christian architecture and that Classical architecture was of pagan inspiration. So the Gothic styles returned (preferably the Early English or Decorated styles of the 13th or early 14th centuries), along with stained glass, benches, choir-stalls, screens and reredoses with the altar, properly furnished, forming the focal point of the interior. Churches were seen again not as mere preaching houses, but as shrines and holy places which must inspire people and bring them to their knees, as well as fitting venues for the celebration of the Holy Mysteries of the Eucharist.

The important thing to remember is that, because the Ecclesiologists were thought to be concerned with architecture rather than ritual, they received considerable patronage from the Anglican hierarchy and people of all schools of thought took notice of them. Many an Evangelical church disposed of its box pews, acquired a new and larger Holy Table, choir-stalls, and maybe even a simple reredos. Even John Charles Ryle – that sturdy Protestant who, before he became Bishop of Liverpool, was incumbent of Helmingham and later of Stradbroke – preached at several re-opening services of Suffolk churches, thus giving his blessing to one of the fruits of the Movement which he loathed. In his own restoration of Stradbroke Church, however, he made sure that 'no fair excuse may be left to any succeeding Vicar for introducing ornaments of an un-Protestant character'.

In Suffolk, therefore, we see the Catholic Revival expressed in the craftsmanship and skill of a variety of architects, builders and carvers. Some are people of national repute, whilst others are the work of local firms. Some of the best Suffolk works of nationally famous architects are:

William Butterfield – Enlarged St Mary at Stoke, Ipswich and restored St Peter and St Gregory, Sudbury, Lawshall, Ringsfield, Ellough and Bacton (where a local artist painted the eastern bay of the nave roof under his supervision).

R. C. Carpenter – Designed St Agnes, Newmarket and the chancel at Harkstead.

William White – Restored Stowlangtoft and Cavendish.

G. E. Street – Restored Freckenham.

Sir G. Gilbert Scott – Designed the round-towered church at Higham Green.

Sir A. W. Blomfield – Designed the two churches of St John the Baptist at Ipswich and Felixstowe.

E. L. Blackburne – Restored Wangford St Peter, Yaxley and Badingham.

J. D. Wyatt – Restored Elmswell and Hadleigh.

Anthony Salvin – Restored Flixton.

Edward Buckton Lamb – Rebuilt Leiston and Braiseworth.

G. F. Bodley – Restored Long Melford tower and Edwardstone and designed the reredos at St Peter, Sudbury.

The Rev'd Ernest Geldart – Restored Langham and Coddenham. This Anglo-Catholic priest was Rector of Little Braxted, Essex.

Charles Spooner – Created the noble and soaring church of St Batholomew, Ipswich.

East Anglian architects also produced work of quality and interest, including:

Richard M. Phipson – Rebuilt St Mary le Tower, Ipswich and Great Finborough, also the tower and spire of Woolpit.

Frederick Barnes – Designed Melton Church and, like Phipson, restored many Suffolk churches.

E. F. Bisshopp – Designed St Michael, Ipswich, the chancel at St Mary at the Elms, Ipswich and many other restorations.

E. C. Hakewill – Rebuilt Thurston and Brantham churches and restored several others. An architect of national repute, he made his home at Playford. His brother designed St Peter, Bury St Edmunds.

Herbert J. Green of Norwich – Rebuilt the churches at Darmsden and Willisham and supervised several tasteful restorations.

J. L. Clemence of Lowestoft – Designed the rebuilt church of St Peter, Kirkley.

J. S. Corder of Ipswich – Restored Swilland, Trimley St Martin, Tuddenham St Martin and several other Suffolk churches.

Fine craftsmanship of the 20th century also graces the churches of Suffolk. Elveden magnificently displays the work of W. D. Caroe, whose sumptuous reredos there would grace a cathedral. The bright and colourful designs of Sir Ninian Comper may be enjoyed at Eye and Lound, and also in the side chapel of Ufford. The sensitive and devotional hand of F. C. Eden may be savoured at Barsham's beautiful church.

Identifying a Catholic tradition, past or present, by looking at church furnishings

CHURCH FURNISHINGS of the 19th and 20th centuries are a useful indication of churchmanship and churches which have been brought directly under the influence of the Catholic Movement provide some of the most beautiful examples of art and craftsmanship in this field.

The restoration or erection of rood screens may be an indication. These emphasise the distinction between the nave and chancel and provide the opportunity for the provision of a rood group, showing Christ crucified and flanked by His Mother and St John, thus replacing what the 16th-century Reformers tore down. Parts of several mediæval screens remain and many of these have been carefully conserved, but several fine new ones have been designed, like those at Rattlesden (1909, to the designs of J. Fellowes Prynne, son of Fr G. R. Prynne of St Peter, Plymouth), Orford (by S. Tugwell and Lawrence Turner), St John, Felixstowe (1910, by Gerald Cogswell) and Hart & Peard's marvellous metal extravaganza (1896) at St Peter, Kirkley. With the coming of the modern liturgy, some screens have been removed, as at Woodbridge and St Mary le Tower, Ipswich. Sometimes, however, there is a hanging crucifix or rood group at the division of the nave and chancel.

Obviously the altar and its adornments were important features for Anglo-Catholics. Modern Catholic worship favours an altar as near to the people as possible and this has been successfully achieved in several Suffolk churches which have retained and developed their Catholic tradition. The Ecclesiologists, however, liked their altars to be raised up at the east end of the sanctuary, in the mysterious distance.

A stone altar was the ideal, its mensa (top slab) having five incised crosses, but this was clearly illegal and was considered to be very "advanced" in the 19th and early 20th centuries. It was achieved, however, at Shipmeadow, Barsham, Kirkley and elsewhere. Some churches had a small stone slab set in the centre of a wooden altar, as Fr Drury did at Akenham. In a handful of others the mediæval mensa, discarded at the Reformation, has been discovered in the floor of the church and has been restored to its rightful purpose, as at Westhorpe, Elmswell and Worlingworth.

Candles on or above the altar were only legally allowed when needed for giving light. Catholics required them for ceremonial use and many churches, including those only mildly sympathetic, dared to introduce them and usually placed them upon a shelf (or gradine) behind the altar. Tall candlesticks, with tall candles (or candles inserted into a white dummy-candle, or stock, to create increased height) showed churches where the Eucharist was regarded as the central Christian service. In many churches there were two, but in more "advanced" churches six were seen above the High Altar, for use at full choral celebrations (in accordance with Western tradition) and two upon the altar itself for said celebrations and offices, and two large standard candles on the altar steps. There was also the Sarum or Old English custom of altars with riddel-posts and curtains. To have a cross upon the Holy Table was greatly frowned upon in the 19th century and some architects got away with the next best thing of setting a stone cross into the masonry of the east wall of a new or restored church so that it would be regarded as part of the architectural decoration. A processional cross was also anathema and a crucifix was even worse, so the presence of a crucifix over the pulpit or anywhere else in the church during the 19th century denoted very "advanced" practices. Churches had to be careful about reredoses (officially illegal in 1880) and it is surprising what Suffolk churches managed to get away with over this (e.g. Brome, Shipmeadow, Long Melford, Swilland, and St Mary le Tower, Ipswich).

More "advanced" churches also acquired a second altar in a side chapel, which was not usually permitted in the early days (Capel were ordered to remove theirs in 1927) and those which were unashamedly Anglo-Catholic and not afraid of trouble often had a third altar, usually for Requiem Masses for the departed. These churches were also equipped with sanctuary lamps, votive lamps, an aumbry for the reservation of the Sacrament, sacring bells and Stations of the Cross. Statues were considered to be no less than graven images and the more "extreme" parishes took great risks in setting them up, not least because they were open invitations to vandals.

Nowadays some of these taboo trappings grace many a central or Evangelical church, where a cross and lighted candles may be seen, together with a credence table, banners and other adornments. Middle-of-the-road churches are often quite beautifully adorned, with sanctuaries richly furnished. Conversely, in line with the modern Western tradition, many "extreme" Anglo-Catholic centres have done away with most of their trappings and the Holy Mass is offered upon a central and sometimes portable plain altar table, adorned maybe with just two stumpy candles!

Seeking out Anglo-Catholic churches is especially rewarding to the church enthusiast, because their custodians have treated them as shrines, to be furnished and adorned with the utmost taste and care, to enhance beautiful and dignified worship, and deliberately equipped to be an inspiration to the visitor who wishes to pray inside them – so their interiors are usually colourful and exciting. A host of symbols, carvings, pictures and aids to devotion, together with burning lamps, well-appointed side chapels and a magnificently-furnished sanctuary, all combine to create a building which is special, sacred, devotional and uplifting and which is indeed the Gate of Heaven in our towns and villages. Several Suffolk churches illustrate this, but perhaps a visit to Mendlesham, Kettlebaston, Ufford, Eye or Lound, will really show how Anglo-Catholics have tried to create something beautiful for God in our Suffolk villages. That great product of the Oxford Movement, the Rev'd Sabine Baring Gould, referring to his restoration of his own little church at Lew Trenchard, Devon, requested that on his tombstone should be inscribed *Paravi Lucernam Christo Meo* (I have prepared a lantern for my Christ). This expresses so simply what so many Anglo-Catholic clergy and lay folk strove to do with our lovely church buildings.

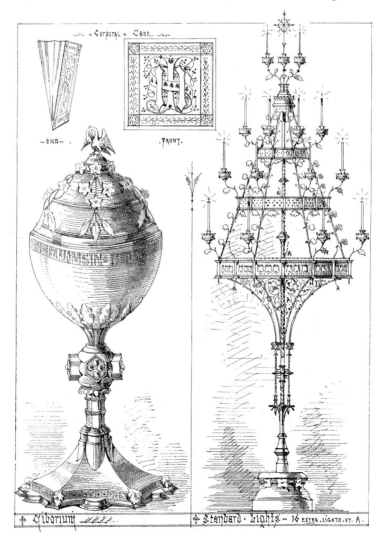

Some Individual Churches

THE FOLLOWING NOTES do not set out to be complete architectural guides to the churches but are simply very brief accounts of how the Movement has influenced them and what can be seen inside them today by those seeking Anglo-Catholic craftsmanship. In many cases such objects as candlesticks, etc., are wisely put in safe-keeping out of service time. Where details of some of their clergy are given, the dates in brackets refer to the years spent in that particular parish. The other parishes mentioned in connection with these clergy are well-known Anglo-Catholic centres at which they served and are selections only from their more detailed biographies in Crockford's Clerical Directory.

BARSHAM – *The Most Holy Trinity*

A simple round-towered church with a thatched roof and thatched lychgate, in an idyllic pastoral setting across a green meadow to the north of the Beccles/Bungay road. The exterior with its round tower and its southern windows of c.1300 has few airs and graces, apart from the unique, trellis-like east window (possibly 17th century) with lozenge-shaped compartments which may be based upon the coat of arms of Sir Edward Etchingham who is buried beneath the chancel. The Suckling family who were lords of the manor and patrons here produced several Anglo-Catholic priests.

Barsham's interior is glorious – a treasure-house of rare and beautiful craftsmanship of varying styles and vintages, all blending to create an atmosphere of devotion and sanctity. Here we have within a mediæval building (parts of which have stood for 1,000 years), 15th- and 17th-century woodwork, also beautiful late 19th- and early 20th-century craftsmanship, much of which has a Baroque flavour and shows what the Catholic Movement can achieve in the beautifying of a small East Anglian church. Much of the work here was provided by the generosity of the Rev'd R. A. J. Suckling (1868-80) and the artistic vision, taste and ingenuity of the Rev'd Allan Coates (1889-1921). The architect for the rebuilding of the north aisle (1908), also the unusual plaster ceiling of the chancel, the aumbry door, the Baroque-style war memorial plaque, much of the stained glass and the general re-ordering of the interior, was F. C. Eden, who was noted for creating interiors with colour, quality and dignity and Barsham is a good church in which to appreciate his work. The unusual wooden arch above the 17th-century screen was painted in memory of Fr Suckling in 1919 and shows St Elizabeth, St Joseph and the dove of the Holy Spirit. The rood group beneath it was fitted into the 15th-century rood beam in 1893. The Chantry Chapel of St Catherine has as its reredos a 16th-century Italian terracotta Madonna and Child with St John the Baptist, which blends into one with its painted surround (by an Italian artist) on the wall.

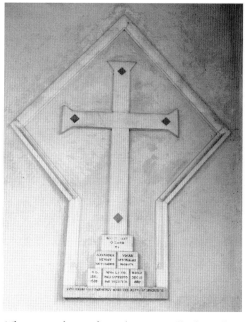

Set in the south wall of this aisle, towards the west, is the original marble cross which William Butterfield designed for the east wall of the Anglo-Catholic stronghold of St Alban, Holborn. When this church received its sumptuous new Bodley reredos in 1896, Fr Suckling had the cross brought to Barsham as a memorial to Fr Mackonochie, his much-loved and much-persecuted predecessor at St Alban's.

The southwest nave window by J. Fisher (who worked for F. C. Eden) is a superb example of its type and shows a beautiful Madonna in a harbour setting, and St Catherine (it is a memorial to Catherine Mary Allan).

The original cross from the East wall of St Alban, Holborn relocated to Barsham in 1896.

The southwest chancel window commemorates the Rev'd R. A. Suckling of Bussage, who died in 1851.

Many of the furnishings to be seen here were acquired by Fr Allan Coates. It was during his time here that the beautiful sanctuary received its present furnishings. Its walls are partly lined with hangings in subdued colours, which form a background for the reredos, designed by Fr Coates himself, incorporating two magnificently carved pillars from All Souls College, Oxford, which support a central canopy. The aumbry door is painted green and gold, with golden rays. It seems that this was never quite finished, as the little memorial inscription on its west side is still roughed out in pencil. The High Altar has a mediæval mensa-slab which was restored to its rightful use in 1900, but was shattered in six pieces by lightning in 1906 and was carefully re-assembled under the direction of G. F. Bodley *(see picture in Clergy section)*. C. E. Kempe filled the remarkable lozenge-shaped compartments of the east window with stained glass.

Fr Robert Suckling.

Tragedy struck again in 1979 when the nave was severely damaged by fire, but the parishioners set to and re-roofed it, making good the damage. This church is certainly worth their excellent care – it is a little gem, where English and Continental styles blend beautifully amidst antiquity, atmosphere and gentle subdued colours in this small Suffolk interior.

The following list of priests who have had the care of Barsham over the past 120 years shows how the Catholic Tradition has been faithfully maintained.

Robert A. J. Suckling (1868-80) – Vicar of St Peter, London Docks (1880-2). Vicar of St Alban, Holborn (1882-1916)

Edward P. Williams (1880-9) – He had been Curate of Chislehurst and St Augustine, Kilburn; also Vicar of St Barnabas, Beckenham. He left Barsham to assist at St Mary Magdalene, Paddington and later at St Matthias, Earls Court.

Allan Coates (1889-1921) – He came here from curacies at the Oxford churches of SS Philip and James and St Barnabas.

Fr Allan Coates.

C. W. Baron-Suckling (1921-43) – He had been Vice Principal of Burgh Missionary College, Domestic Chaplain to Bishop King of Lincoln and Vicar of Alford, Lincolnshire before coming to Barsham.

Geoffrey Ingle Soden (1944-57) – He was curate at St Alban, Holborn and later Rector of St James, Wednesbury.

Harold A. Raymond (1957-9) – Curate of St Peter, Folkestone and St Peter, Kirkley. Chaplain of Clewer House of Mercy and Vicar of Swanmore, Isle of Wight. After leaving Barsham he was Parish Priest at Bacton, Norfolk, Burnham on Crouch, Arkesden in Essex and Duxford in Cambridgeshire.

Fr Baron-Suckling.

Francis E. Westmacott (1960-75) – Previously Vicar of Hepworth and Rector of Harkstead and Erwarton. He conducted Barsham's services for several years after his retirement.

BURY ST EDMUNDS – *St John the Evangelist*

This remarkable church was designed by William Ranger of London and built in "white" Woolpit brick in 1841. Its lofty spire dominates the skyline on the north side of the town. This church, in the style of the period immediately before the Gothic Revival, has rather bold architecture in a development of the Early English style, with large lancet windows. The 160-foot tower and spire are very stately and compelling. The interior was considerably altered by J. D. Wyatt in 1875/6. A striking feature is its wooden groined ceiling, painted blue and studded with gold stars above the sanctuary.

Today we enter a church which has been gloriously made to live – hardly an easy task with a large and cumbersome building of this period. Its internal stonework has been painted in bright colours. In 1945/6 the east end was beautified when Faith Craft were engaged to colour the reredos and to enrich it with statues and also to adorn the High Altar with a new Rood crucifix and six candlesticks. The aumbry in the Lady Chapel was dedicated in 1943.

St John's has become a beacon of Anglo-Catholicism in West Suffolk, although its development was very gradual. The pew system was abolished in 1872 under the Rev'd S. Holland and during the 1870s an early celebration of the Holy Communion was tried on certain Sundays, but often there were no communicants. The Rev'd C. H. G. Baker (1878-84) introduced a weekly 8.00 am celebration, and a daily celebration (which later lapsed) began in 1882. The Rev'd Thomas Stantial (1884-1906) invited Fr C. E. Osborne of St Agatha, Landport and H. A. Kennedy to conduct a Mission in the parish. Canon E. W. Adams (1907-37) re-started the daily Eucharist upon his arrival. He also had a monthly Choral Eucharist and introduced eucharistic vestments. He was a member of the English Church Union and several of their festivals were held here. It was the Rev'd W. A. C. Ullathorne (1942-51) who established a weekly Sung Mass and perpetual Reservation of the Sacrament. He also introduced the full ceremonies for Holy Week and Easter. Incense was used for the first time at St John's in 1947, and at the Church Union Festival in 1949 the first High Mass in the history of the church was sung. Subsequent parish priests have maintained the church's tradition and today it is a much loved and much used centre of contemporary Catholicism.

CAPEL ST MARY – *St Mary*

St Mary's stands above the old village street and has an attractive and satisfying "village church" exterior, with fine 14th- and 15th- century windows. Inside there is dignity, colour and devotional charm. Its fine old roofs shelter a host of lovely things which have been introduced to aid devotion and to enhance the tradition of worship which became firmly rooted here over two long incumbencies.

Fr A. C. Johnson (1878-1920) installed the distinctive bridge-like

Capel St Mary – the interior pre 1920.

rood beam and its figures. The Lang family of Oberammergau carved these and the large angels with musical instruments, which peer out from the chancel roof, in pearwood. Fr Johnson imported the striking reredos from a Belgian church and Maurice Keevil painted this at a later date. His final gift, in 1920, was the glass in the east window. After having witnessed its installation he remarked to his churchwarden 'now I have done all that I wanted to in the Church'; he went home and died that night. On the day of his funeral his son, Fr Vernon Johnson (a Mission Priest of the Society of the Divine Compassion, who later became a Roman Catholic), placed the Oberammergau crucifix from the Rectory Oratory upon the altar, where it remained for 40 years.

A set of Stations of the Cross, which are fine German steel engravings and were once in the nunnery at Claydon also came from this Oratory; a beautiful modern set has now replaced these.

Fr Johnson was Patron of the Living and he had great influence in the village, where he worked hard and greatly loved the people, instituting shoe, clothing and hospital clubs for them. He never took a holiday, believing that a day out of Capel was a day wasted. During his time, linen eucharistic vestments were worn and incense, although not used ceremonially, was burned in copper bowls on each side of the altar.

Fr A. C. Johnson.

Fr Vernon Johnson was born in the Rectory and took an active interest in this church. Princess Marie-Louise of Schleswig-Holstein offered him a stone altar for the south aisle, but the Diocesan authorities refused to permit its installation.

Fr J. H. M. Robertson (1920-51) came here from the staff of St Alban, Holborn. Having married, he had no choice but to leave the clergy house life there. During his time, the Chapel of St Edmund was made (to the designs of Howard Brown) in the south aisle; its east window (by F. C. Eden) is Fr Johnson's memorial. The Willis organ was moved to the west end in 1927, when Bishop & Son constructed its fine case. Fr Robertson is remembered as a quiet, calm and holy man, whose careful teaching in church, school and village built up a committed congregation. He instituted daily Mass, Reservation and full Catholic privileges here, making Capel as "advanced" as any church in East Anglia. He was plagued by persecution, not only in the 1926 court case (see p. 161), but people also remember the many makeshift thuribles which were manufactured because the real one was repeatedly stolen, and the occasional heckling of his beautiful outdoor processions which took place, either through the village or across to Little Wenham, accompanied by incense, banners and girls with streamers.

Today the interior is bright and colourful. The focal point, beyond the distinctive rood-beam and its figures (which caused so much trouble in 1926) is the magnificent traceried and painted High Altar with its tabernacle, above which soars the rich Gothic tracery of the noble Belgian reredos. Tasteful modern craftsmanship may be seen in the sanctuary lamp, the large wooden statue of Our Lady, the Stations of the Cross, the colourful kneelers, and the panel of stained glass in the south aisle (by G. Maile) representing the Risen Christ – the 15th Station of the Cross.

The interior has changed as Capel church life moves on. The side chapel is now an open space near the nave altar and further plans for development are afoot. However, the heavenly orchestra still looks down from the chancel roof, the Sacred Heart statue and our Lady of Walsingham still adorn the nave, and the building reflects a vibrant worshipping community.

Large Crucifix outside the tower.

CHEVINGTON – *All Saints*

There is an inviting and atmospheric exterior to the church, which is set in a quiet and picturesque corner, away from its main centre of population. We see Norman work here and the tower (built c.1500) received its distinctive and rather odd top stage in 1822. The interior combines good mediæval craftsmanship (eg font, nave roof, benches and 14th-century chest) with dignified modern work of c.1983, which has transformed the chancel for modern liturgical requirements. This interior underwent several alterations during the 20th century and provides an interesting record of change in Anglo-Catholic furnishings.

For many years the patronage was in the hands of the White family and the Rev'd A. Keble White (1908-26) had got himself into trouble in the 1880s for certain illegal furnishings (including the use of candles and an altar stone) in his church at Burley, Hampshire. Shortly after his arrival here the interior was transformed. Benches in the nave replaced the box-pews and the altar was enlarged and furnished with a cross and candlesticks. An elaborate traceried screen was erected in front of the narrow chancel arch and extended the full width of the nave and above it was placed the organ; Fawcett & Atkinson of Cambridge were the architects for this work. The organ and screen were removed in 1937. Clearly Keble White was a priest in the tradition of the Tractarians,

View of nave with screen and organ in situ – pre 1937.

although he was by no means extreme. Mrs White, however, appeared to have more "advanced" ideas than her husband and upon his death in 1926 she gave the patronage of the living to the Guild of All Souls and appointed the Rev'd R. H. Nottage (then at Kettlebaston) as the new parish priest. Shortly after leaving Chevington she became a Sister in a Roman Catholic order.

Fr Nottage was more extreme than his predecessor and shortly after his arrival here he made several changes. The Holy Communion was called "Mass" and was celebrated daily. Six candles appeared upon the High Altar, crucifixes were set up in the church and the use of incense was introduced.

These innovations were like a red rag to a bull to certain Chevington Protestants, and one Mr Dyson led a movement in opposition to them. He welcomed Mr Kensit's Wickliffe Preachers to the village and these folk, together with a Mr Vercoe Abbot of Ipswich, held forth at open-air meetings in the village, attended by several Primitive Methodists, other folk from the surrounding parishes and a few members of the parish church who disliked the changes.

Fr Nottage wrote to the Bishop asking for his support and expressing his genuine concern and anxiety because of this bad feeling. The Bishop replied, regretting the action of the Wickliffe Preachers, and also several neighbouring clergy expressed their sympathy. Scurrilous messages were discovered written upon the altar, the candles and the crucifixes in the church, and correspondence appeared in the local press complaining about eucharistic vestments and prayers for the departed at Chevington. In a survey (which few parishioners took part in) 34 church members indicated that they were happy to leave the running of the church to the Rector, whilst only 4 expressed a wish to have "Protestant Services" in the church. In time the Wickliffe Preachers' protests subsided, Mr Abbot became a Primitive Methodist, a few folk left the church and Fr Nottage began to build up a good and committed congregation. In 1930 he published a book entitled *The Village Eucharist* based upon his work in his two Suffolk parishes. He began a duplicated handwritten parish newsletter in 1929. In 1932 he was appointed to the living of All Souls, Clapton; he later became Rector of Corringham, Essex and his closing years were spent as Parish Priest of Rawreth, near Rayleigh, where he was buried. The Catholic tradition for which he fought at Chevington continued there.

In 1961 a very long High Altar and six new candlesticks were placed at the east end, but in 1983 these were removed and we now see, in a central position in the

chancel, a much smaller stone altar on a central shaft and corner pillars, designed in the French Cistercian Romanesque style. In the north-east corner a circular stone pillar supports the metal Sacrament House which replaced Fr Nottage's tabernacle. A wooden crucifix and six simple candlesticks stand on the sill of the east window. Three 15th-century benches and Chevington's wonderful mediæval chest stand in the whitened chancel, which is otherwise cleared of furnishings. It all looks rather bare but gloriously uncluttered and atmospheric, and All Saints certainly has the feel of a holy place.

The Sacrament House.

CLAYDON – *St Peter*

Claydon's cruciform church stands proudly on the brow of a hill overlooking its village and the Gipping Valley and forms a distinctive landmark for some distance from the west. A lane climbs up to its churchyard entrance, beside which is the high wall that Fr George Drury built around his grounds. From the churchyard are glimpses of the flint garden walls and gazebo that he built and near the churchyard wall, to the south of the chancel, is the grave of this priest who was the centre of such turbulence in the 1860s and 1870s. It is difficult today to imagine the fiery scenes which took place here – all is now peaceful and quiet, and a pilgrimage to this country churchyard is well worthwhile.

The long-and-short quoins in the western corners of the nave tell us that Christian worship has taken place upon this high and holy spot for a thousand years. The pretty tower and north porch are 15th-century; the chancel was rebuilt and the transepts, with their steeply pitched roofs, added in 1851-52. The architect for this work was R. M. Phipson, but doubtless Fr Drury told him exactly what he wanted – his own handiwork may be seen in the glass of the east window (with its picture of Our Lady of Walsingham, made long before her shrine was revived), the elaborate stone pulpit, the tower pinnacles and the chancel décor. Henry Ringham made the benches, reading desk and the wooden vaulted crossing roof. The nave roof and font are mediæval.

St Peter's is now in the care of the Churches Conservation Trust, who were unable to rescue some of its vandalised furnishings, so we can only imagine its interior in the late 19th century, with a simple painted rood screen and rood group above, the chancel, with its intricately stencilled walls, the High Altar (which had a small inset stone mensa), and the six tall candles which backed it. A tiny chapel was made to the east of the north transept.

Drury's terrier of goods unashamedly catalogues the possessions of this small church during his time here, which gives us an idea of the items that he introduced. These include:

'High Altar, set of frontals, side Altar with frontals, etc., chasubles; one set of the ecclesiastical colours of the Western Church, with dalmatics, stoles, albs, burses, maniples, five corporals and six purificators, eight altar candlesticks, two crosses, eight flower vases, three copes, three cottas, two surplices, eight cassocks, one thurible, one processional cross, one banner, one Prayer book, one Missal, one Ritual, one Bible, one bell in tower, Sanctus Bell in chapel, one server's bell'.

Fr Drury was Rector here from 1846 until 1895 and was succeeded by Fr Ansell Jones who had served his title at St Martin, Brighton. Under him Claydon was still definitely Catholic, but in a less advanced manner – doubtless the Bishop of Norwich and certain parishioners were relieved! He notes in his register the occasional choral Eucharist, celebrations on Thursdays and Saints Days, and Stations of the Cross during Holy Week. The English Church Union held festivals here, and there was a Solemn Procession around the churchyard at All Saints-tide. He died in 1927, aged 84 years. Fr L. B. C. Newell (Rector 1931-56) had a monthly Sung Eucharist with incense and he revived the Blessing and Distribution of Palms which had ceased here after Fr Drury's death. Claydon folk now worship at Barham Church, which contains several items from Claydon Church. Sadly, Claydon's High Altar was destroyed, but Shipmeadow's altar, with its marble mensa slab, has replaced it and it fits beautifully.

The final resting place of Fr George Drury in Claydon churchyard.

DENNINGTON – *St Mary*

One of Suffolk's most interesting and fascinating churches, this treasure house of superb and unspoilt fittings contains exquisite craftsmanship from mediæval times up to the 20th century. All of these combine to give this church an unforgettable interior, where the unspoilt atmosphere of antiquity, beauty and devotion is a delight to many a church-crawler. The way in which people of the 20th century have restored it and made it beautiful is of interest here, because this work is the direct result of the Catholic Movement.

At the turn of the century, the interior was rather drab and lifeless. In the sanctuary stood the plain and unadorned Stuart Holy Table, with a kneeler at its north side. What was later discovered to be a rare and valuable mediæval pyx-canopy (one of only four in England) was used as a doorstop for the vestry door, and the Lady Chapel was filled with box-pews.

The first real changes were made by Fr George Douglas Castleden (1921-44) who came here from St Andrew, Fulham and set about restoring the sanctuary according to the Western Tradition. The Stuart table was lengthened and adorned with frontals and a curtain was fixed to the lower part of the east window to form a background for six candlesticks, equipped with tall stocks (or dummy candles) into which the real candles fitted. The central altar cross was dwarfed by the candles and was placed upon a square box which was veiled to look like a tabernacle, but was not used as such because Fr Castleden discovered the true purpose of the vestry door-stop, had a pyx made and suspended it beneath the mediæval spire-canopy above the altar. He began Reservation here in 1927 and the great day was celebrated by Vespers of the Blessed Sacrament, which was shared by Fr Drake and some of his people from Ufford. It seems that the Rector was greatly influenced and encouraged by one of his Fulham curates, the Rev'd W. De Lara Wilson, who was one of the organisers of the 1933 Anglo-Catholic Congress. Under Fr Castleden there was a weekly Sung Mass; there were also Rogation processions, the Veneration of the Cross on Good Friday, Palm processions, Christmas Midnight Mass and proper observance of all Feast Days, including Corpus Christi.

His successor was Clement Mallory Ricketts (1945-55) who was also the Bishop of Dunwich. He was a moderate High Churchman who retained the Sung Eucharist as the main Sunday service. Fr Castleden had done little about the fabric of the building and the Bishop instigated a timely restoration of the church under the guidance of W. H. Randoll Blacking, who designed the present Sarum arrangement of the sanctuary. The restoration continued under the Rev'd James Gilchrist (1955-66) – an expert on mediæval churches and their

furnishings and an acknowledged authority on church plate. He instigated much of the internal refurbishment to the designs of Eric Sandon and using mostly East Anglian craftsmen. This work included a new High Altar, the making of the Lady Chapel and the restoration of its aumbry to contain the Holy Oils, also the re-equipping of the Bardolph Chapel for use as a chapel, with a new stone altar and striking bronze and copper candlesticks each side of the tomb-recess. Fr Gilchrist also had a new pyx made to fit beneath the ancient canopy; when the old pyx was opened some particles of the Blessed Sacrament were discovered inside it. These he reverently consumed, although they had been placed there by Fr Castleden in 1945, as Bishop Ricketts did not use the pyx. During Fr Gilchrist's time here, sacramental worship and Catholic teaching were maintained, but without being extreme. He moved to Norfolk in 1966 leaving this grand church intact, beautiful, and in many ways a model of what can be done to make a mediæval church with an array of furnishings from past ages really live.

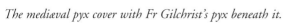

The mediæval pyx cover with Fr Gilchrist's pyx beneath it.

ELMSWELL – *St John the Divine*

Elmswell's glorious 15th-century tower stands proudly upon its ridge, looking across the A14 to Woolpit's noble Victorian spire. St John's has been a flourishing Evangelical church since c.1920 but for some 60 years before then it was a beacon of the Catholic Revival, whose influence created so much of the beauty that we see here today.

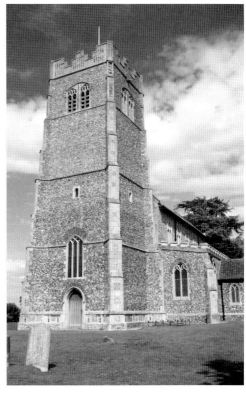

When the Rev'd Dr William Henry Colbeck Luke arrived in 1863 the south aisle had just been restored to the designs of John Henry Hakewill. Dr Luke came here from a curacy at Chislehurst; he paid for the chancel to be thoroughly restored and the north vestry built, to the designs of R. J. Withers, and also gave an organ to the church in 1864. Through his influence a new rectory was built in 1864 and a school and schoolhouse in 1865. In 1872 the nave was thoroughly restored and a new north aisle was added to the designs of J. D. Wyatt. The shields adorning the nave roof, and the painting on the reredos (showing the pelican in her piety) were executed by the Rev'd William Francis, curate-in-charge of Great Saxham (who published diocesan maps of England and Wales and wrote a book of anthems and their composers). It was probably then that the High Altar, with its stone mensa slab upon a wooden framework, was made. The top surface of the slab has been smoothly cut and marked with the five crosses, but the underside is rough-hewn, so it may be that the mediæval altar-slab was rediscovered and re-used.

Fr Luke was a member of the Society of the Holy Cross and in 1877 he organised a priests' retreat at Elmswell, conducted by Dr Edward King, later to become Bishop of Lincoln. He left in 1878 to be Vicar of St Matthias, Earl's Court. He died in 1892.

The Rev'd W. A. C. MacFarlane (1878-93) had been Curate at St Giles, Oxford. He left in 1893 and gave the beautiful wrought-iron chancel screen, crowned with the eagle of St John, which was erected the following year. The

Rev'd James Hipwell (1893-1908), who was a member of the Society of the Holy Cross, had served several London curacies, including St Stephen, Lewisham, St Paul, Lorrimore Square, and St Augustine, Kilburn and had been Chaplain at the All Saints Sisterhood, Margaret Street. He loved working in towns and cities and had hoped to spend the rest of his ministry as an assistant curate in London conducting missions and retreats. He had refused eight offers of country livings, but when his health broke down in 1887 he spent two years as curate-in-charge of Woolpit and a further two years as vicar of Leavenheath, before coming to Elmswell.

He was a hardworking and caring parish priest who was a fine teacher, as his letters in his parish magazine show. Very definite Catholic teaching was given, although the services were not extreme. Holy Communion was celebrated at 8.00 am on Sundays, Holy Days, and Tuesdays and Thursdays, with occasional choral celebrations. Sung Matins and Evensong took place each Sunday. He advertised that during the octave of a festival there would be an additional 10.00 am celebration for the aged and infirm.

There were many church activities, including a Glee Club conducted by the rector, a Guild of St John the Divine for boys and girls and meetings of the Confraternity of the Blessed Sacrament. The restoration of the ancient churchyard cross (with money given by Mrs Luke) was largely to his design. Fr Sandys Wason served his title as curate here from 1894 to 1897, but remained in deacon's orders as the Bishop of Ely refused to priest him because of his extreme churchmanship. He returned to preach at the dedication of the Henry Jones organ in 1901.

Fr Hipwell retired to Hove and was followed by the Rev'd John R. George, who had been vicar of Northmoor, Oxon. After he left in 1919, Elmswell's churchmanship changed.

EYE – *St Peter and St Paul*

This large and magnificent church, with its sumptuous 101-foot tower, is set in a quiet and idyllic corner of its small Suffolk market town. A fine mediæval church of this size and architectural merit provides wonderful scope for Catholic worship and Eye's bright and spacious interior has been gloriously and tastefully adorned, using all that is best in mediæval and modern traditions of furnishing.

Dominating the interior is one of Suffolk's grandest late 15th-century screens with exquisitely painted mediæval panels. This has been majestically transformed by Sir Ninian Comper who, in 1927, using Rattee & Kett of Cambridge as contractors, added the rood-loft and splendid rood figures, thus restoring its mediæval glory and colour. The design and colouring of the old and new work blend perfectly. Comper also designed the font cover with its delicate openwork, the five hanging sanctuary lamps, the six High Altar candlesticks and the glass in the east window, which is a memorial to the Rev'd John Polycarp Oakey, whose robed figure is seen on the right hand side, kneeling before St Polycarp. Miss Maude Tacon gave this glass in memory of their long and close friendship.

What had been a very 'Comper-ish' sanctuary, with richly draped High Altar and walls lined with silk hangings, was tastefully transformed in 1969 to enable the modern liturgy to be celebrated with ease. The modern work, in limed oak, comprises Communion rails, organ case, altar and reredos, with a Polish granite gradine supporting Comper's six tall candlesticks. The small stone mensa let into the High Altar was consecrated by Pope Pius XII for Fr Donald Rea. This remarkable priest, who was Vicar here for 32 years, is commemorated by the beautiful figure of the Virgin and Child, by Lough Pendred, which fills the mediæval tomb recess in the north aisle. The south chapel is equipped with a stone altar and modern Sarcrament House, in which the Blessed Sacrament is reserved.

As with many churches, the development of the Catholic tradition at "High Eye" was very gradual in its early stages. During Canon Donald Campbell's time (1879-93) the Holy Communion was celebrated once or twice per month, and the parish was very missionary-minded, supporting both the SPG and the CMS. The Rev'd A. J. Spencer (Vicar 1893-1904) established celebrations of the Holy Communion on Sundays and Saints Days and the Rev'd John Pritchitt (1904-1917 and formerly curate at All Saints, Cheltenham) introduced occasional choral celebrations, daily celebrations during Holy Week, Three Hours Devotion on Good Friday and a pair of Gospel lights.

The High Altar c. 1910 with the Bateman-Hanbury memorial reredos erected in 1908 by Harry Hems of Exeter. Much of it is still in place although hidden from view for many years.

It was the Rev'd J. P. Oakey (1917-27) who instituted a monthly Choral Eucharist, kept most of the Western Feast Days, including Corpus Christi, and the Assumption of Our Lady and was probably encouraged in all this by some of his more extreme curates. Fr J. R. Vincent, who came here from Mendham, had Matins and Mass on alternate Sundays. He introduced palms on Palm Sunday, also the Paschal candle, and during his time (1927-34) Comper's glorious re-ordering of the interior was completed and dedicated, most of the work having been financed by the Patron, Miss Maude Tacon.

The year 1934 saw the beginning of Fr Donald Rea's long ministry here. He had been a lecturer at Chichester Theological College and his remarkable pioneer

The Interior after 1929. The Comper transformation is almost complete save for the introduction of the east window.

The High Altar in the late 1950s, by now sporting a 'big six' and Tabernacle for Reservation of the Blessed Sacrament.

work whilst at Eye in promoting mutual friendship between Canterbury and Rome did much behind the scenes to bring the two Churches closer together. He became a personal friend of the saintly Pope John XXIII, who presented him with his own personal Breviary.

Eye's tradition has been maintained under subsequent vicars. Comper's exquisite colour and artistry still shine out in this wonderful church, where ancient and modern craftsmanship blend beautifully and the aroma of incense greets the visitor as he enters by the great west door.

Fr Donald Rea.

The High Altar today: the careful reordering of the Sanctuary allows Mass to be celebrated either Ad Orientem, or Versus Populum. Comper's 'big six' now stand on a black marble gradine with an insert of liturgically coloured cloth.

FELIXSTOWE – *St John the Baptist*

This stately red-brick building by Sir Arthur Blomfield (nave and aisles 1895, chancel and Lady Chapel 1899, with its 120-foot tower and spire added in 1914 to the designs of Charles Blomfield), stands in the highest part of the town and the spire is visible for miles over land and sea. This is surely one of East Anglia's best examples of "Seaside High Church"; it inspired the late Sir John Betjeman, who encapsulates the feel of its interior in his poem, "Felixstowe" when he says, 'I hurry past the cake-shop's tempting scones, bound for the red-brick twilight of St John's'. The latter is certainly true – apart from the west window and the clerestory windows there is only one window in the building that does not contain a saint or biblical character in richly coloured glass (nearly all by Powell & Sons) bathing the interior in devotional dusk. St John's is lofty and spacious, dignified and prayerful, with walls of exposed red brick. Beyond Gerald Cogswell's beautiful screen, with Christ crucified, flanked by his Mother and St John above it, is the stately chancel and sanctuary. The sanctuary floor is paved with mosaic and the High Altar is backed by the subdued colours of the alabaster-framed reredos (designed by J. Powell) which was the gift of Canon A. Pretyman of Great Carlton, Lincolnshire and shows the Last Supper, but with Judas absent.

To the south is the Lady Chapel, with the aumbry where the Blessed Sacrament is reserved. The carved figures of the Archangel Gabriel and of Our Lady guard the chapel's entrance and Saints Felix, Fursey and Edmund – the saints of Suffolk – look out from its east window.

The Exterior in 1898 before the addition of the Chancel and Tower.

The Interior before the addition of the Chancel in 1899.

The High Altar, c. 1950.

St John's was always of a different tradition from the Evangelical parish out of which it was carved, and from the very beginning the Holy Communion was celebrated every Sunday, Thursday and Saints Day (in surplice and stole, with the eastward position) and clear basic sacramental teaching was given. For some reason the Rev'd W. Done Bushell, the tall bearded Chaplain and House Master of Harrow School, was on the Building Committee. This noted Anglo-Catholic was also Lord of the Manor of Caldey Island in Wales and it was he who invited Fr Aelred Carlyle to found his Anglican Benedictine Community there. He presented a pair of candlesticks for St John's altar and proposed that all its sittings should be free of pew rents.

In 1899 the Vicar, the Rev'd J. Munday (1895-1907) met with opposition when he petitioned for his new chancel, side chapel and certain furnishings. The Chancellor of the Diocese objected to two points: he disliked the proposal that the High Altar should be raised upon several steps; and he saw no need for a second altar in the chapel. Fr Munday was summoned to appear before him and by persuasion was able at length to win the day. The second altar was granted because the Vicar convinced the Chancellor that this would save the church £50 per year in heating and lighting for small services. The elevated High Altar was in the end allowed when the Vicar cleverly pointed out that this enabled the congregation to see clearly the manual acts of the priest at the Holy Communion – something that all anti-ritualists considered to be essential. Fr Munday had been Vicar of Bardney, then Rector of Clee and Cleethorps, Lincolnshire and was a friend of Bishop King of Lincoln. He left St John's to become Vicar of Stanwell, Middlesex.

The Rev'd A. Evered Stantial (1907-21) had been Rector of Bacton since 1890 and was the son of the Rev'd Thomas Stantial of St John, Bury St Edmunds. He became a familiar figure in the town, wearing his cassock and biretta. He had made it clear to the Church Council before his arrival that if he came, he would use Eucharistic vestments here. By 1914 there was a choral Eucharist every Sunday, a Eucharist every day, and a host of guilds and societies for parishioners. During his time here the screen arrived, as did the beautiful silver sanctuary lamp, some of the stained glass windows, vestments, frontals and banners. A fine musical tradition, which was to last for many years, was also developing here.

Although a convinced Catholic, Fr Stantial had little sympathy with the idiosyncrasies of some of the more extreme element of the Catholic wing of the church and he wrote in his parish magazine against priests muttering the Consecration Prayer and certain young men reading books of devotion instead

Canon W. Cocks with the Choir of St John, Felixstowe.

of following the service. He exchanged livings in 1921 with the Rev'd William Cocks of Frome Woodlands, Somerset and wrote in the magazine commending his successor as 'a definite Catholic, reverent and hard-working'.

Fr Cocks had sound training from his childhood mentor, Fr Francis Mills of Broadstairs and St Thomas, Finsbury Park. He presided somewhat autocratically over a 40-year era that was to make St John's one of the leading parish churches in the diocese. In 1937 there were 719 people on the Electoral Roll, 200 Free Will Offering subscriptions, over 250 Mother's Union members, a Bible Class of 115 and a Men's Society of over 70. A man of tremendous talent in music, drama, practical organisation and pastoral work, he engendered tremendous enthusiasm and vitality. He maintained the church's tradition but was very much a Prayer Book man; real religion to him was what he called "Spiritual Catholicity" – he hated Papalism and was totally loyal to the Church of England and her teaching.

The gentle and saintly Canon George Tidey (1962-75) was a Mirfield man who had done incredible work in Burma as an SPG missionary priest. A wonderful teacher and skilled confessor, he lovingly and gently weaned many of the congregation away from Choral Matins and into the Parish Communion, which developed during his time here. During the time of Fr Kenneth Francis (1976-97), St Thomas More was placed in a Lady Chapel window and since the arrival, in 1998, of Canon David Lowe, seven new bells have been added and a beautiful set of Stations of the Cross, etched in slate by Anthea Chalkley in 2005, enhance the interior with craftsmanship from our own time.

IPSWICH – *St Bartholomew*

This noble building, which is surely one of the finest of its period in East Anglia, was designed by Charles Spooner to be an inspiring and dignified setting for Catholic worship in all its fullness. It was consecrated in 1895 and its west end was completed in 1907. The red brick exterior has a vast all-embracing roof which rises above the streets of terraced houses surrounding it.

The interior is glorious – it is spacious, lofty and flooded with light. The vast unbroken nave and chancel, the broad arcades and the soaring roof far above, create a feeling of space and dignity. There is no Victorian fussiness either and all this allows for the church to be furnished on a grand scale without appearing cluttered. The skeleton is unashamedly mediæval Gothic, yet other traditions of design blend in beautifully and all is work of superb quality with a tasteful use of colour. Of special note are the handsome font and pulpit of alabaster and green marble, the huge Stations of the Cross, made at the studios of the Sisters of the Church, the War Memorial altar by F. C. Eden in the north aisle, the statue of Our Lady of Walsingham in the south aisle, the hanging crucifix above the chancel steps, and the large statues of Our Lady and St Bartholomew which flank the chancel entrance. Most of what we see here are gifts to the church, often as memorials to past members.

The chancel has good 20th-century woodwork (some by Ernest Barnes of Ipswich) and the organ is one of the finest in the town. The focal point is the

High Altar backed by its tabernacle, dignified gradine, crucifix and six tall candlesticks. Above the curtained backcloth and canopy (by William Morris & Co.) is a single large circular window filled with beautiful tracery. The Blessed Sacrament Chapel and its impressive reredos was designed by H. Munro Cautley and erected in 1925 as a memorial to the church's first Vicar. Its colourful adornments provide an imposing setting for the Sacrament and a devotional corner where people may come to pray.

The Interior c. 1916 and before the addition of the Blessed Sacrament Chapel in 1925.

Throughout its history St Bartholomew's has been a leading centre of the Catholic Movement; the caring, teaching and evangelistic ministry of the first Vicar, Fr George Cobbold and his Curate, Fr Charles Curtis, formed its tradition. From this grew a high standard of ceremonial, preaching, music, work and witness. Several missionaries, priests and nuns have been nurtured here, a host of guilds have flourished and always St Bartholomew's has been at the forefront of the Movement. Fr Cobbold (1894-1915) and Fr Curtis (1899-1915) formed a magnificent team, and worked tirelessly in this parish of terraced houses to bring Christ and his Church to the people, working in the best traditions of the great urban priests like Fr Wainright of St Peter,

Fr Cobbold.

The eastern end of the Nave and the Sanctuary in the late 1950s.

The High Altar in the late 1950s.

Statues of St Bartholomew and Our Lady.

The Blessed Sacrament Chapel in the late 1950s.

The Requiem Altar by F. C. Eden.

London Docks and Fr Dolling of St Agatha, Landport, both of whom preached from St Bartholomew's pulpit. These foundations were built upon by subsequent vicars. Fr Claude Powell's memorable ministry here (1916-46) saw the formation of a variety of parochial guilds, spectacular outdoor processions of witness at the Patronal Festival and the beginnings of the parish's strong links with the development of pilgrimage to the Shrine of Our Lady of Walsingham. The 1936 pilgrimage programme

A view of what is believed to be an early side altar.

began with Low Mass and Holy Communion at St Bartholomew's at 6.30 am followed by breakfast in the Church Hall. Solemn Mass took place at 11.00 am at Walsingham ('the *English Hymnal* and veils are usual', pilgrims were informed), followed by a procession to the Holy House. The afternoon included intercessions and the bathing of the sick and finished with Vespers and Benediction at 5.00 pm. The party then returned to Ipswich, arriving about 9.00 pm.

St Bartholomew's continues to be a spearhead of the Catholic Movement in Suffolk. Its tradition has been maintained by Fr S. J. Matthews (1946-51), most of whose ministry was spent in Australia, where he was consecrated Bishop of Carpentaria in 1960; Fr W. A. C. Ullathorne (1951-64) who came here from St John, Bury St Edmunds and left for the parish of Lakenheath; Fr Daniel Gooderham (1964-71), who later served at Rattlesden and at St Michael, Beckenham; Fr D. K. Woolner, who came here from Claydon and remained here until his untimely death in 1983; Fr John Burrows who retired in 2003; and Fr Paul Carter the present parish priest.

Fr W.A.C 'Clement' Ullathorne.

IPSWICH – *St Mary at the Elms*

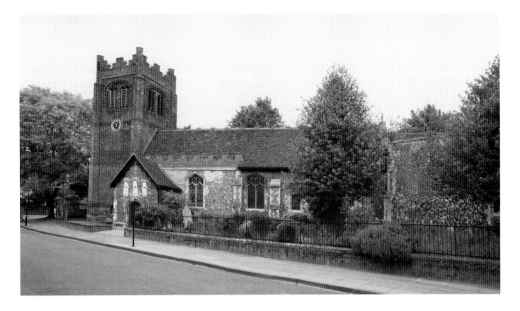

This is a small and greatly loved oasis of calm and quiet amidst the bustle and commerce in the western part of the town centre, which was once in an area of small streets of terraced houses. St Mary's is a little Norman church with a fine Tudor brick tower, which was extended in 1883 by a new chancel to the designs of E. F. Bisshopp. The Norman doorway and its ancient door are set in a leaning wall, revealing its great age.

During the daytime, this little shrine is open and is greatly used; it is usual to enter and actually to find people praying. Although this is the Anglo-Catholic town-centre church, its furnishings are refreshingly simple and unprepossessing. Colour has been used judiciously, particularly to pick out the emblems surrounding the chancel arch. The removal of superfluous seating has made the chancel spacious and devotional. Six tall candles surmount the plain wood-fronted High Altar, each side of the tabernacle veil, which gives a central splash of colour in just the right place. The blocked east window provides a perfect frame for the great Crucifix which fills it. At the east end of this north aisle is the dignified altar and reredos (1948) of the Chapel of the Holy Apostles. Behind the western screen, beneath the tower, is a small and intimate chapel which was furnished by Fr Crowther Alwyn; it contains a small brick and stone altar, above which is the statue of Our Lady of Walsingham.

In 2002 Robert Mellamphy's beautiful statue of Our Lady of Grace of Ipswich was placed on the south side of the nave, forming a Shrine that is prayed at by

Anglicans, Roman Catholics and other Christians. The Diocesan Bishop, the "Flying Bishop" a Roman Catholic priest, a Methodist minister and a Moslem woman all took part in its dedication service.

No vast or spectacular building this, but there is much of beauty here and St Mary's does have its own very endearing way of getting people to their knees!

It was Fr Percy Youlden Johnson (Vicar 1918-50) who moulded the tradition here. Within a year of his arrival a weekly Choral Eucharist and a daily Eucharist were established. Incense was first used in 1920, a new altar and its adornments arrived in 1921 and by 1924 the Blessed Sacrament was reserved in the church. Fr Johnson's service registers make fascinating reading; his remarks provide an interesting commentary on the weather, the war and a host of national and religious events. He was Chaplain to the Actors Church Union and he formed a very lively parish Amateur Dramatic Society.

Fr Vivian Crowther Alwyn, who succeeded him, developed and considerably advanced the tradition of St Mary's and the church has been a vibrant and much-loved centre of Catholic devotion and teaching ever since. Its doors are still open, the Mass still celebrated daily and people still use it as an oasis of prayer.

The Interior in 1922 showing what Fr Johnson had achieved in four years!

IPSWICH – *St Mary le Tower*

The handsome civic church of Ipswich, set in its quiet green churchyard, is a haven of peace in the busy town centre and is a superb example of all that the Ecclesiological Movement proclaimed. It was almost totally rebuilt by stages between 1850 and 1873, although much of the stonework of the arcades, the font, the pulpit and a few other features survive from the former church. It had been handsomely furnished for 18th-century worship with box-pews, galleries, etc., which the restorers triumphantly cast out! The architect was R. M. Phipson, who designed a lofty building, embodying pure Gothic architecture of the Decorated and early Perpendicular periods. The grand southwest tower with its soaring spire is the main glory of the exterior. The interior has a dim devotional dusk, created by the rich stained glass in the windows. The lofty nave and chancel enhanced by soaring arcades, the encaustic tiles in the floors, the fine woodwork and the glass, all embody the Ecclesiologists' ideal of what a church should look like; so we must imagine it with its former rood screen and the walls with courses of black decoration and rows of encaustic tiles beneath the windows – all now painted over.

The sanctuary, which was designed by Somers Clarke and painted in 1895 by Hamilton Jackson, forms a rich climax with its magnificent reredos in memory of Canon Turnock.

St Mary's was the first Ipswich church to be influenced by the Oxford Movement. The Rev'd William Nassau St Leger (1838-61) upon his arrival unashamedly declared his entire accordance with the *Tracts for the Times* and was heard to remark that in his opinion the Reformation did as much harm as good. It seems that he was not always in residence here as an 1855 Directory states that at that time he was Military Chaplain in Corfu, whilst St Mary's was under the care of a curate. He certainly combined his love of the Army with his

Tractarianism as he held services at the Tower for the Armed Forces and installed Regimental Colours there. He was an eloquent extempore preacher and his opponents said that his discourses were more like Roman Catholic homilies than good Protestant sermons. His "Puseyite" tendencies caused some excitement in the town, although his innovations were very moderate. He introduced a surpliced choir and was known to have intoned parts of the service.

His successor was James Robert Turnock (1861-90) who had served a curacy at Christ Church, Albany Street, St Marylebone, one of the early outposts of the Movement. He was only 34 when he arrived at St Mary's but was a skilled preacher and teacher who was described as a 'High Churchman of the older school', who 'fought the good fight for the Catholic Faith in Ipswich'. At the Tower he introduced the daily offices and several weekday communion services.

The Rev'd Ythil Barrington (1890-1904) started a daily Eucharist here in 1894 and had frequent Choral Eucharists on Sundays. The English Church Union Anniversary services were held here in 1895, the preachers being Fr Charles Wakefield of Woolverstone and Fr Harry Wilson of St Augustine, Stepney.

So was established here a tradition which was definitely Catholic from the very early days of the Movement; it never advanced at later periods to the more extreme stages of Ritualism but has remained to the present day, coupled with a first-class musical tradition and a very special ministry to the Borough of Ipswich.

KETTLEBASTON – *St Mary the Virgin*

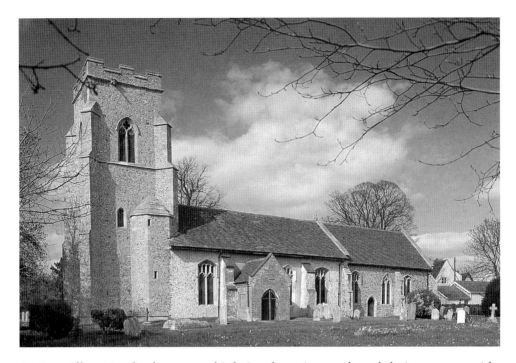

A tiny village in the lanes, set high in charming and undulating countryside, between Hitcham and Preston St Mary. Its mediæval church is delightful, containing Norman work in its font and nave walls, a doorway of c.1190 and beautiful 14th-century work in the tower and the chancel, with its fine east window, sedilia and piscina. This little shrine in its idyllic setting was for many years a thriving centre of advanced Anglo-Catholicism in West Suffolk. It was at one time the scene of near riots, but it also attracted large regular congregations which included people from the surrounding parishes and children and Sisters from the Home of the Holy Childhood which was situated in the parish.

St Mary's today is still greatly cherished by the people of its small community, although the services here today are a little more familiar to the majority of Anglicans than were some of the services in years gone by! The interior has a compelling and unforgettable charm, where space, light and colour help to create an exquisite atmosphere of devotion. Even before entering, the pilgrim senses that there must be something special here because in the mediæval niche in the south-east chancel buttress, behind a pair of small wrought-iron gates, is a painted alabaster carving of the Coronation of the Virgin – a reproduction of one of the four famous Kettlebaston alabasters, discovered here in 1864 and now in the British Museum.

Inside, St Mary's exudes atmosphere – it is the perfect combination of mediæval antiquity, rustic charm and the unashamed richness of its Catholic furnishings, which have been preserved intact. The eye is drawn to the blaze of colour in the recently re-instated tabernacle above the High Altar, and to the rood screen and reredos, both of which were designed by the Rev'd Ernest Geldart, the priest-architect of Little Braxted. The screen, which is surmounted by the Rood Group, has six painted panels showing English Saints, painted c.1950 by Enid Chadwick of Walsingham. At the centre of the reredos is a carved scene of the Annunciation, which is flanked by saints. Our Lady appears again at the

The Interior, pre 1930.

summit of the reredos but this time she is crowned. Both screen and reredos have a really authentic mediæval flavour and quality.

On each side of the chancel arch are small altars. That to the north is the 17th-century Communion Table upon which is a statue of the Sacred Heart, beneath a canopy given in 1939 and between two pairs of very Gothic-looking metal candlesticks. The southern altar has Our Lady's statue (given by a daughter of Fr Powell of St Bartholomew, Ipswich), set beneath a very lovely canopy. Both altars have sanctuary lamps with hanging tassels.

The High Altar is of stone; it was made c.1950 by Saunders of Ipswich to the design of Fr H. C. Butler, the Parish Priest. It is supported upon pillars that are enlarged imitations of those in the 14th-century sedilia. On the gradine above are six Baroque-style candlesticks flanking the tabernacle.

The first Kettlebaston Rector of note was the Rev'd W. S. Sellon (1894-1911) who was trained at Chichester Theological College, had been Curate of Swanmore, Isle of Wight and incumbent of parishes in Herefordshire. During his time the church interior was transformed to Fr Ernest Geldart's designs and the worship became very advanced and included the use of vestments and incense, much to the fury of local Baptists. The chancel was restored, its floor was raised and the old communion rails found their way to Rattlesden church.

Fr Edward Scarlett (1911-12) had been curate at St Alban, Bordesley, St Faith and St Michael, Wandsworth and St Peter, Streatham. During part of his time here Fr T. Stowell Jackson, who had been Curate-in-Charge of Woolverstone and later helped at St Faith, Stoke Newington, assisted him. Fr J. F. Todd (1912-21) had served curacies at St Margaret, Aberdeen, St Chad, Haggerston and St Anne, Hoxton and this was his first and only parish. Fr R. H. Nottage (1922-6) came here from curacies at St John, Bury St Edmunds and Great Finborough and left to be Rector of Chevington. When he arrived here it appears that there was no house for him, so he lived and slept in the church's small sacristy for a time until a wooden bungalow was built for him near

Fr Nottage, parish priest 1922-6.

the Home of the Holy Childhood (the former Rectory). The church building when he arrived was in a poor condition and through his efforts it was restored.

Restoration of the nave roof in 1922.

He was a hard-working and popular priest, who ministered to a full church each Sunday. After the Sunday evening service of Vespers and Devotions, people were invited to the Rectory for a social gathering, with refreshments, music and games. He was succeeded by Fr Richard de Bailleul Coussmaker (1926-8), who had served curacies at Holy Redeemer, Clerkenwell and St Nicholas, Guildford and left to become the Parish Priest of parishes in Staffordshire.

Fr Harold Clear Butler's long ministry here lasted from 1929 to 1964. He came here having been curate at St Agnes, Bristol, Falmouth, St Michael, Walthamstow and six years at St John, Clerkenwell. A committed Papalist, Fr Butler maintained a system of worship at Kettlebaston that was clearly Roman rather than Anglican and this was probably the only church in the diocese at that time which had advanced so far. He was very much an individual, with a high regard for his priesthood and for the type of Christianity that he represented. His Sunday services were usually Mass at 11.00 am and Vespers at 3.00 pm. The great annual event during his time at Kettlebaston was the Assumptiontide Vespers and Benediction, which was followed by a garden party. He was more than a little suspicious of the Church of England in general and had little time for what he called "High Churchmen". He disliked having "State" notices pinned up in his porch and refused to keep registers of his normal Sunday and weekday services. He maintained that Fr T. C. Elsdon of St John, Clerkenwell did not keep registers either and that these were quite unnecessary, insisting that they were probably the invention of 19th-century High Churchmen who liked to write down all the new services that they had introduced in their parishes! The only entry he did make reads '1933, October 2nd, 2.30 [pm] – visitation of Archdeacon of Sudbury. Abortive. Archdeacon, finding no Churchwardens present, rode off on his High Horse.'

He was a man of great artistic taste, with an understanding of beauty in mediæval churches. It is thanks to his skill and care that Kettlebaston Church is believed by many to be the ideal of what a country church should be. Amongst the works which he commissioned were the gate to the rood loft stairs, the magnificent decoration of the reredos and screen, the two small altar lamps, the carving and gates for the external southeast niche and the new stone High Altar which he designed. He personally, and with considerable skill, cleaned the old and tasteless paintwork from the south door, the sedilia and the 17th-century Communion Table and he renovated the monument on the north sanctuary wall, using an ordinary lead pencil to bring out the lettering.

Ill health forced his retirement in 1964 and, of course, it was not possible for a tiny parish like Kettlebaston to have another Rector of its own. It has been placed with various other parishes over the years. A former parish priest, Fr Brian Findlay, formerly Vicar of St Augustine, Tonge Moor, Bolton, revived some of the very special traditions of this beautiful and much cherished church.

KIRKLEY – *St Peter*

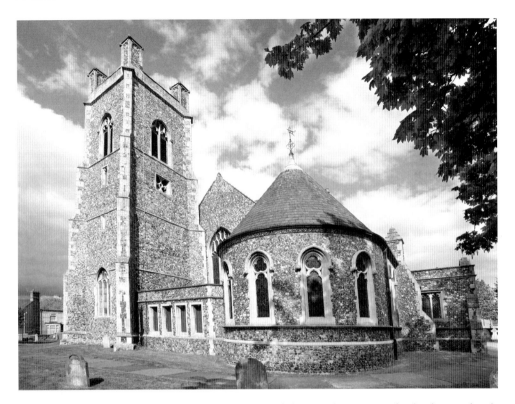

St Peter's, a noble and distinctive product of the Gothic Revival which is sedately positioned at the southern end of Lowestoft, has been a beacon of Anglo-Catholic worship in the Lowestoft area for many years. During the 17th century the mediæval church had reached such a decayed state that from about 1680 Kirkley folk used Pakefield Church and Kirkley's priest shared the conducting of the services there. When a mid-18th century Vicar failed to do his share of the work the Vicar of Lowestoft told him that if he refused to officiate in Pakefield Church, 'I will build you a church at Kirkley, and there you shall officiate'. He was as good as his word and Kirkley's old south aisle was restored for use in 1750. A photograph of this church's interior just before the present church was built, shows a humble building, with the Lord's Prayer, Creed and Commandments on the east wall and a cross above the altar – very different from the fine church which replaced it and which grew between 1875 and 1893. The Lowestoft architect, J. L. Clemence, designed it and Thomas Porter (also of Lowestoft) added the apsidal baptistry in 1892. It is a grand building, with a noble flint-faced exterior, incorporating the mediæval tower. The interior is inspiring and contains superb craftsmanship. Its remarkable feature is the amazing and intricate painted wrought ironwork by Messrs Hart & Peard of Drury Lane and amongst the finest of its type in any church in the country. Sir A. Blomfield supervised the designing of the chancel screen (1896) and the baptistry screen. The font cover and the remarkable clock at the west end are also superb wrought ironwork; a clock in Rouen inspired the latter. All this metalwork, also the baptistry and the grand four-manual organ (Brindley & Foster 1881, enlarged in 1891 by Norman & Beard) are amongst the host of generous gifts by Edward Kerrison Harvey, who was the Lay Reader at this church for many years. There are two fonts here – the ancient one was brought from the ruined church of All Saints, Gillingham, Norfolk.

The High Altar and Sanctuary before 1926.

The High Altar is 12 feet long and its large mensa-slab of red stone, in three parts, was installed in 1887. The present stately and colourful reredos was designed by Canon Gordon Roe, Rector of Acle and formerly of Leiston, and made by L. Howard & Son of Norwich. Some of the paintings of the saints were clearly inspired by the mediæval screen at Ranworth. This reredos and the six tall Baroque-style candlesticks came in 1927. The sanctuary lamp is 18th-century and may be continental. The Blessed Sacrament is reserved in a homely little chapel to the north of the chancel.

The south chapel altar was the High Altar of Kirkley's former Mission Church of St Matthew and the rood figures from St Matthew's screen are now in the baptistry. This church still stands in Clifton Road, nearer the town centre – it is an attractive timber-framed building by Bottle & Olley of Yarmouth, built in 1899. In its heyday it was the scene of much activity and was an effective and caring Catholic centre in the poorer part of the town. It closed about 1921.

The Interior, before 1926.

The first Vicar of the new church, the Rev'd W. W. English (1875-85), had an 8.00 am celebration of the Holy Communion every Sunday, on Saints' days and monthly after Matins. His successors – the Rev'd E. T. d'Eyncourt Jesse (1885-90), who published a book of prayers for the departed, and the Rev'd Charles Tregenna (1891-8) were both members of the Society of St Osmund, which existed to promote the restoration of the Sarum Use into the ceremonial of the English Church. They instituted and used here the English colours and liturgy, together with sound sacramental teaching, although it seems that Fr Jesse used Gregorian chants whilst Fr Tregenna changed to the *Cathedral Psalter*. The new Trinity vestments given in 1896 were made of dark crimson figured satin, with cloth of gold orphreys on a blue background – all very rich, beautiful and very Sarum!

Kirkley folk doubtless noted a difference, however, when the next Vicar, Fr R. Henry Cockayne (1898-1911) arrived. He made the change to the

Western use, with Western colours and ceremonial. On Sundays in 1900 at St Peter's the Choral Eucharist followed Matins, whilst at St Matthew's it preceded it. The parish was clearly a thriving one, as there was a daily Mass in both churches, and a minimum of five Sunday services in each church.

Fr G. R. P. Preston (1920-45) came here from St Mary, Potters Bar, whose large and magnificent church was built during his time there. It is not surprising therefore that Kirkley's handsome reredos is of such high quality. By 1948 at St Peter's there were three Sunday masses (8.00 am Low, 10.00 am Sung and 11.00 am Solemn) and Evensong was followed by Devotions. Kirkley continued as a beacon of advanced Anglo-Catholicism under Fr A. C. Barwood (1957-61) and it was only when the parish of St John's, Lowestoft was united with it in 1974 that the present more moderate Catholic tradition was introduced.

LEISTON – *St Margaret*

The 15th-century tower and 13th-century font are almost all that remain of Leiston's mediæval church – the rest was rebuilt in 1853 in a remarkable original and distinctive manner to the designs of Edward Buckton Lamb (the architect of Eye Town Hall, Braiseworth Church, St Martin, Gospel Oak, London and several other very eccentric buildings). It was built for Leiston's Evangelical Vicar, the Rev'd John Calvert Blathwayt, whose parish was developing into a small industrial town and whose small church was attracting large congregations of people who came to hear his forthright Gospel preaching. He wanted a large preaching auditorium which would seat over 800 people and so Lamb designed one of Suffolk's most exciting 19th-century churches – a commodious cruciform building with low side walls and lofty gables, crowned with a roof which is an essay in Victorian genius, particularly where the radiating timbers converge at the crossing, above the vast central space.

Mr Blathwayt's successor was a man of very different ideas. He was the Rev'd Berney Wodehouse Raven (1874-1909) and, although by no means an extreme Ritualist, his preachers' books and service registers provide an interesting guide to his gentle and gradual nurturing of an Anglo-Catholic tradition here. By 1880 there was a celebration of the Holy Communion on every Sunday and Saint's Day and the choir was robed. Various ornaments for the sanctuary arrived for Easter 1884 and by 1887 there was a "High Celebration" of the Eucharist on festivals and at least once per month, with two celebrations every Sunday, and Solemn Evensong became the custom at festivals, where brass instruments were used to enhance the grandeur of the music and the service concluded with a procession and solemn *Te Deum*.

The Bishop of New Westminster preached here in 1888, vested in cope and mitre (a great rarity in those days) and in that year the sanctuary was re-ordered, decorated with colour and the "proper ornaments" placed upon the altar. In 1890 eucharistic vestments were worn for the first time. Canon Raven's beautiful marble and mosaic memorial plaque is near the organ; it shows him wearing vestments and carrying the chalice.

His successor, the Rev'd R. Gordon Roe (1909-15), was an artist and designer of church furnishings (including Kirkley's reredos). He maintained Leiston's Catholic tradition and equipped the church with new choir stalls, a rood beam and a side chapel. After his departure, St Margaret's became more "Central" and it was not until 1973 that the

The High Altar in the 1920s.

Eucharist once more became the central act of worship each Sunday and vestments were again worn; the Blessed Sacrament was first reserved in the side chapel in 1974.

The visitor to St Margaret's today will find an impressive and distinctive interior with a dignified sanctuary, where stencilled colouring still adorns its arch and six candles stand above the High Altar, although the painted reredos has gone. The east window has colourful glass by C. E. Kempe and there is fine 20th-century glass in the north transept by Margaret E. A. Rope of Blaxhall (who also designed windows for St Benedict, Ardwick and St Augustine, Haggerston). An alabaster statue of Our Lady of Lorraine suckling the Holy Child stands in the Lady Chapel and a beautiful triptych of Our Lady of Leiston (painted by the Marquis D'Oisy) may be seen in the north transept. The interior of this eccentric church has been sensitively and tastefully transformed to the designs of Simon Merrett (architect and church warden) with a central altar beneath the crossing, dedicated in 2006.

LOUND – *St John the Baptist*

The simple unprepossessing exterior of this small round-towered church on the Lothingland Peninsula gives little hint of the exquisite beauty and magnificence to be found inside it. People call it the "Golden Church" and indeed its interior does shimmer with gold and many other fine colours – a splendid example of how the Catholic tradition, coupled with the skill of Sir Ninian Comper, can transform a small country church.

Lound is rich in elegant and beautiful woodwork, seen in its splendid openwork font-cover, grand organ case and sumptuous rood and rood-loft. In 1914 Comper created here something of what a mediæval interior must have looked like before the Reformation. Our Lady, St Salome and St Elizabeth look out from their painted panels above the stone Lady Altar to the right of the screen. The sanctuary beyond shows so gloriously the beauty of Comper's work and his ability to create a superbly proportioned, dignified and devotional setting for worship. The altar is furnished in the Sarum style, but with six candles. Its riddel-posts, crowned with golden angels, carry rich dossal curtains, where we see

The High Altar, c. 1960.

"Comper Pink" predominating. He had them made in Spain where he procured scarlet silk, which he then had bleached in the sun until it was just the shade that he required.

Here we see (and smell) the Catholic tradition in all its richness and beauty still working in a village church. It was the Rev'd B. H. Lynes (1908-17) who was the driving force behind the 1914 refurbishing, who gave the rood-loft and who developed a moderate Catholic tradition here. Fr L. P. Howes (1917-26) built upon this, instituting a weekly Sung Mass and holding a Mission, conducted by the Cowley Fathers, in the parish in 1920. He left to become Chaplain to the Sisters of the Church at Kilburn and was followed by Fr K. J. K. Corbould (1926-36), who had been trained at St Matthias, Earls Court and under whose leadership Lound became a very advanced church, with Benediction, celebration of Our Lady's Assumption, Easter Eve ceremonies, etc. Amongst the later incumbents was Fr Robert Linton Shields, D Mus (1943-58) who had worked at St Mark, Lakenham, Norwich, St Peter, Vauxhall and had been Chaplain and a Lecturer at King's College, London.

MENDLESHAM – *St Mary*

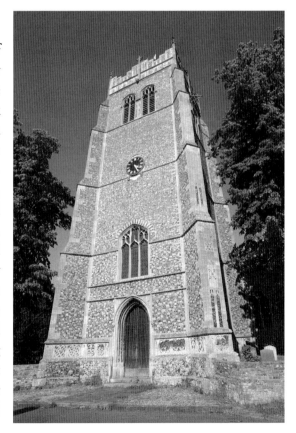

Here is a fascinating example of what has been done, especially during the last 30 years, to make a gem of a mediæval Suffolk church live. Mendlesham is a church-crawler's paradise: superb architecture, a grand flint-panelled tower and porches, 17th-century font-cover and pulpit, mediæval benches, Sanctus bell turret, brasses and grand proportions, to say nothing of the unique parish armoury in the chamber above the north porch. All this could make a church a very interesting museum of ancient things, but through taste and care over recent years, St Mary's, with all its treasures, has become one of the most colourful, lived-in and devotional churches in the county, mainly through the efforts of its present parish priest who has a great love of old churches and their furnishings, and of the Church of England's Catholic heritage.

The church has a grand exterior and a superb setting, with its west door opening onto the village street, and the churchyard has an unusual number of beautifully tended graves. The ancient Sanctus bell turret is now equipped with a small bell which was once in use at the Vicarage. The magnificent tower, 84 feet high, has occasionally been the setting for the letting off of fireworks into the sky from its roof on special festivals. Beside the main entrance, beneath the noble north porch, is the 16th-century font from Rishangles Church, now beautifully cleaned and restored for use as Mendlesham's Holy Water stoup!

The interior is magnificent, colourful and flooded with light, where tasteful work of our own times blends with fine craftsmanship of past ages to create an exciting and inspiring shrine, which is saturated with the atmosphere of prayer and devotion. Along with Mendlesham's own furnishings are benches and glass from the redundant churches of Southolt and Rishangles, and items from other closed churches. The interior is studded with shrines, candles and votive lights, all very evocative and worthy, and mostly installed during the early 1980s. The little aumbry for the Holy Oils, beside the tower arch, has a wooden surround that reflects the style of the font cover, and above the chancel arch is a colourful rood group.

The south porch with its grand mediæval roof and entrance arch is now Holy Cross Chapel. The church's chantry book of the departed is placed upon its altar and its walls have dramatic paintings by Cyril Fradan. At the east end of the north aisle is the Lady Chapel, with the church's Jacobean altar table, and Our Lady's statue (1965) is in its 15th-century niche. The Blessed Sacrament Chapel (1982) has a striking altar, made up of ancient stones from Mendlesham and Rishangles churches, topped by Mendlesham's mighty mediæval mensa slab. In a reliquary recess in its western side are relics of St Vincent and St Victorinus, which are indicated by a votive lamp standing on the floor nearby. The aumbry in the east wall has a tasteful crown canopy and a golden veil.

The eastern section of the nave has been cleared for the nave altar (designed by Jack Penton, 1982), on a central plinth which has a simple "XP" motif. The small mensa slab set into it is from St Augustine, Haggerston. Of more recent date are the metal Stations of the Cross on the walls.

The spacious chancel is cleared of superfluous seating and the priest's doorway now frames the beautifully carved statue of Our Lady of Walsingham (1982);

nearby is a stand for votive candles. The east wall is lined with simple light wood panelling, made in 1962, against which the frontal of the High Altar gives a splendid blaze of colour. The six candlesticks and candles are not tall ones, but they fit well into their surroundings.

This church is the centre of much activity throughout the year. Mendlesham has its Boy Bishop, and its May Queen is crowned annually. Processions are still known to wend their way through the village streets, fireworks ascend into the night sky from the church tower, and other glorious and godly celebrations take place. It has become a centre in Suffolk for the Papalist wing of Anglo-Catholicism and has been regarded as a refuge by those who in all conscience find themselves unable to accept the ordination of women.

The Rev'd E. R. Manwaring White (1861-77) had the church restored by Ewan Christian. The preacher at its re-opening was the Rev'd G. Cosby White, Vicar of St Barnabas, Pimlico. The Rev'd Edmund Richard Manwaring White was vicar here from 1910-32 and was succeeded by Fr P. T. E. Wareham who came here from Westhorpe; he advanced the tradition here and did much to restore the fabric of the church. Fr Herbert Pearce (1954-5) had been curate at Kirkley and rector of Foxearth, Essex and was later vicar of St Chad, Manningham, Bradford. Fr Frederick Shaw CR, came here from Horbury, Yorkshire and was succeeded in 1957 by Fr A. C. Housego, who was a member of the Society of the Divine Compassion and had been curate at St John's, Tue Brook, Liverpool. Fr Philip Gray arrived in 1974 from a curacy at St Clement, Leigh-on-Sea and has remained here.

NEWMARKET – *St Agnes*

A small but very noble church on the Bury Road, where the population of horses is said to be higher than that of humans, this remarkable building, with its distinctive bell-turret and spirelet, was opened in 1885 and was designed by R. C. Carpenter. It embodies all the beauty, colour and dignity that the Ecclesiologists hoped for in a church building and it was clearly erected for worship according to the principles of the Oxford Movement.

It was built by Caroline Agnes (hence its dedication), Duchess of Montrose, who lived nearby, as a private chapel which was open for public worship and as the memorial church to her second husband, W. S. Stirling Crawfurd, whose remains (originally buried at Cannes in 1874) were re-interred behind this church in 1885. The Duchess was a Scottish Episcopalian who was clearly of the Catholic tradition and she certainly spared no expense in building and adorning this little shrine. She and Bishop Woodford of Ely had much correspondence over the splendid marble bas-relief sculpture by Boehm that was to be erected above the High Altar, and which dramatically portrays the taking into heaven of St Agnes above the Coliseum in Rome. The Bishop was highly suspicious of this (it has more than once been mistaken for the Assumption of Our Lady) and he refused to allow it, so for a time it had to remain at the side of the chancel, covered by a cloth. It seems that Bishop Alwyne Compton, who became Bishop of Ely in 1886, became reconciled to the sculpture because he consecrated the completed church in 1887, when the Rev'd Alfred Sharpe became its first Vicar. Before this he had been Chaplain to the Duchess and Curate-in-Charge of the church, which was a district church within the parish of Exning.

Fr Sharpe had been Curate of the London churches of St Andrew's, Wells Street and St Peter's, Vauxhall. He left St Agnes in 1888 and in 1895 he became Vicar of St Peter's, Vauxhall. He was followed here by the Rev'd W. Colville Wallis (1888-1934) who had been Curate of Holy Trinity, Ely. The Rev'd C. L. Buckwell (1935-8) came here from a curacy at All Saints, Clifton, Bristol; he left to become Vicar of J. H. Newman's former parish of Littlemore, Oxford and was later Vicar of St Michael, Croydon. Following the long ministry (1939-66) of the Rev'd H. D. P. Malachi, the parish was united with St Mary, Newmarket.

Although St Agnes now steers a middle course in churchmanship between the Catholicism of St Mary's and the Evangelical worship at All Saints, it is a rewarding and unforgettable building. Its interior is small, yet is appears to be so much larger and loftier than it actually is. Its adornments are lavish and dignified, with exposed red brick and glazed tiles lining the walls, fine wood-carving, and the High Altar, with its six candles set against one of the most amazing east walls in the county. Immediately above the altar and forming a reredos is the light coloured Renaissance-style bas-relief of the Assumption of St Agnes, above which are three majestic double wall arches, giving the impression of a triforium passageway and framing six colourful saints, worked in Italianate mosaic, giving a truly Byzantine feel. Above these, the upper section of the wall, to its apex, is lined with mosaic work - a little High Victorian shrine, like a jewel, and unique in East Anglia.

NEWMARKET – *St Mary*

Set sedately away from the town centre, its 14th-century tower, with little corner bell cage and slender shingled spire (like a tall "Hertfordshire spike"), together with the south arcade and a c.1300 piscina recess, are about all that survive from a very extensive Victorian transformation and enlargement which was done by stages between 1857 and 1887, involving the Newmarket architects John Francis Clark and William Holland and later Percy Holland & Son. The interior is colourful and dignified, yet feels homely and lived in. Whilst light floods into the nave and aisles, the chancel is bathed in devotional dusk. Lovely 1930s

windows by Christopher Webb allow the light in, whilst the 19th-century glass in the chancel filters it somewhat and C. E. Kempe & Co has c.1908 glass in the south aisle. The chancel aisles form eastern chapels (that on the south for the Blessed Sacrament). The north chapel screen in 1920 was designed by Fr Henry Young as a war memorial and has carvings of St George and St Joan of Arc, representing England and France. It was modelled on the mediæval screen at nearby Landwade. The chancel arch is imposing and the east window is set high, creating a lofty and dignified feel and forming the perfect setting for the High Altar. Much of the east wall is covered by 20th-century traceried panelling, with statues of Our Lady (with a pair of candles and a votive lamp) and of Jesus the Good Shepherd flanking the east window. The lower woodwork has a cornice of vines, etc. and incorporates the reredos with central canopies over the altar cross above and the aumbry beneath, flanked by six candles and guarded by gilded trumpeting angels.

During the time of the Rev'd John Imrie (1880-90) the Holy Eucharist was celebrated every Sunday and on occasional weekdays, but it was Fr H. B. Young (1904-20) who moulded the tradition which was to remain at St Mary's to the

Then and now: the High Altar in times past (top) and present (bottom).

present day. In his service registers he noted all festivals and most Sundays in Latin and he instituted a Sung Mass (occasionally called "Messe Solennelle") which followed Matins every Sunday. He had been trained at St Giles, Reading, St Paul, Knightsbridge and Holy Trinity, Sloane Street. Fr John Prankerd (1921-39) continued and developed the tradition, and under him Candlemass and Palm Processions, and the Mass of the Presanctified on Good Friday were introduced. Fr Isaac Morris (1939-45) came here having been Vicar of Lakenheath for 20 years and from the start of his ministry here he recorded a Mass every day of the week. Daily Mass, incense and full Catholic privileges continued here under Fr H. C. Eves (1945-51), during whose time the Sung Matins ceased and the church was visited by the Choristers of St Mary of the Angels and their Founder, Fr D. Morse Boycott. Fr Morris Russell (1951-9), replaced the non-communicating Sung Mass at 11.00 am with a 9.30 am Parish Mass. Fr Kenneth Child (1959-69) came here from St Augustine, Tonge Moor, Bolton and was later Archdeacon of Sudbury; and subsequent rectors have maintained the tradition here.

SHIPMEADOW – *St Bartholomew*

The atmospheric interior with F. C. Eden's tryptich reredos.

Twenty years ago this little redundant Norman wayside church was a sad sight, where the hoofmark of the vandal was very much in evidence. The pretty war memorial lychgate, with its crucifix, tottered at a nasty angle and the ancient church was forlorn and neglected. A grassy path leads from the Beccles to Bungay road to the entrance of this small building on its knoll, overlooking the Waveney Valley, with its rustic 15th-century tower attractively laced with Tudor brick.

The church was closed in 1980, although for some years the abandoned interior still contained the 15th-century font and screen-base, 17th-century chest and Royal Arms of King George III, and many of the fittings made for it as a result of the Catholic Revival were also still in place. The Stations of the Cross and the six High Altar candlesticks had been removed, but the statues of Our Lady and St Bartholomew still looked out from the niches flanking the chancel arch. The High Altar was still vested in its white frontal, the empty tabernacle above it was still veiled and other fittings remained, looking as if they were just waiting to be used. Behind the altar was the dignified painted triptych reredos, designed by F. C. Eden and given in 1897, together with the marble mensa slab of the High Altar, by Fr Robert Suckling in memory of the Rev'd Maurice Shelton Suckling who was Rector here from 1850 to 1894. On the reredos was a central rood group with the Angel Gabriel on the left-hand section and Our

Fr Claude Powell.

Lady attractively portrayed with the dove of the Holy Spirit pulling at her hair on the right. It has now been tastefully and sympathetically converted for use as a house, but the beauty and proportions of the interior have been ingeniously preserved and the building is still beautiful.

Fr James Halliburton Young was Rector from 1894 to 1904. During this time a reporter from *The Record* came to spy out and to condemn in print a Sunday Solemn Mass, performed with "all the trimmings". His successor, the Rev'd Claude Powell, left in 1916 to become Vicar of St Bartholomew, Ipswich. The Rev'd John Clegg had been Curate at St Ives, Huntingdonshire and Headmaster of Lowestoft College; he left in 1929 for St Mark, Oulton Broad.

Small though this parish was, the last Rector to reside here (Fr Gerald Manson, 1929-40) had a daily Mass, and the Sunday services were Low Mass at 8.00 am (for about 4 to 6 communicants), Matins at 10.15 am, Sung Mass at 11.00 am, Catechism at 2.30 pm and Evensong at 3.00 pm. There were 22 Easter communicants in 1939. After it was linked with Barsham in 1940, the number of services was of necessity greatly reduced.

SWILLAND – *St Mary*

This is a tiny church that is full of surprises; the lower stages of its very distinctive tower are of Tudor brick, whilst the unique upper stage is a homely and not unattractive extravaganza of timber-framed brickwork with dormer windows, and crowned by a thin copper spirelet. This and the porch were designed by J. S. Corder and erected in 1897. A large Norman doorway gives access to the remarkable interior, which is colourful and has great character. The focal point is the altar, with its magnificent painted and gilded reredos, carved with figures of the Apostles, saints and angels. The central tabernacle has now gone, although the recess where it was placed still remains.

From earlier periods the mediæval roof, 17th-century pulpit and Royal Arms of Queen Anne survive, but most of the beautiful things to be seen here are from the late 19th century and this little interior is a splendid specimen of a church that has been gloriously furnished for Catholic worship – a Tractarian period piece.

The Rev'd C. H. Gaye (1874-82) came here from St Matthew, Ipswich, where he had been labelled as a "Puseyite", but the more advanced Catholic worship was brought to Swilland by the Rev'd P. C. Bicknell, who came to this quiet Suffolk village in 1882 having been trained through curacies at three beacons of the Movement – Holy Cross, St Pancras, St Margaret, Liverpool, and All Saints, Margaret Street, London W1. He was Swilland's first young Rector for many years and with all the keenness of a young priest in his first living, he set about

The Interior in the early 20th century showing the richly decorated east wall and chancel ceiling.

restoring his little church. Its interior walls were covered with stencilled paintings, angels and inscriptions, and the ceiling was painted with foliage design with the words of the Magnifcat inscribed beneath the roof cornices.

Fr Bicknell's earnestness and zeal won the hearts of Swilland folk, who were largely behind him in his efforts – they loved, trusted and confided in him and he showed an uncommon tenderness and intense affection for them. He was a well-read man with a love for beauty and reverence in worship and a hatred of anything slovenly, and it is therefore little wonder that his services attracted large congregations, including people from the surrounding villages, and that Swilland folk really warmed to this young man who had 'an almost feminine tenderness and intense affection'. He had never been a physically strong person and because of a throat weakness he was advised to go abroad for the winter of 1886. On Advent Sunday of that year he preached his last powerful sermon to his sad and tearful congregation, many of whom feared that it would be their last meeting. He then travelled to his father-in-law's house in London before starting off for the south of France. Here he suffered a haemorrhage and died on 12 December 1886, three days before his 33rd birthday, leaving a young wife and two small children. His body was brought back to Swilland and was buried in the spot near the church porch which he had chosen himself.

The Rev'd R. H. Faulconer (1892-7) was responsible not only for the work on the tower and porch, but also for many of the present furnishings, including the altar frontals and the beautifully embroidered banner, which is embellished by many small glass beads; also the painted organ case, the making of the vestry under the tower and the richly-coloured glass windows in memory of his predecessors at Swilland (both St Richard and St Felix have the face of Bishop Edward King of Lincoln). He also had the splendid reredos with its rood group and twenty saints erected in 1894 (probably to J. S. Corder's design). During his time there were 50-60 Easter communicants and about 40 at the three Ascension Day eucharists, the first of which began at 5.00 am.

His successor, Fr L. J. Thomas, maintained the Catholic tradition here and used vestments and incense, but did not have his predecessor's dynamism and attendance dropped somewhat. Sadly he lost his 35-year-old wife in 1911 in tragic circumstances and he collapsed and died on the church path in 1916. Fr Charles Spencer (1916-8) restarted the Sunday School and Women's Guilds, provided new red vestments and instituted the English Hymnal and Rogation processions. He exchanged livings with the more moderate Fr Francis Keane who remained at Ashbocking and Swilland for 42 years.

UFFORD – *St Mary of the Assumption*

Few visitors to Ufford fail to come under its spell. Who could resist this picturesque and endearing village, set in the lush Deben Valley and full of rural charm, with a gem amongst churches, idyllically set, with a superb exterior. The village stocks are by the gate, the tower is handsome, and there is beautiful architecture in the windows and handsome flushwork in the porch. Amongst the treasures inside is what many believe to be the finest and most beautiful font-cover in the world.

This unforgettable corner of Suffolk has been, for the past 100 years or so, one of the county's best-known Anglo-Catholic centres and the tradition thrives here still. The church is saturated with the prayers and devotion of centuries and its mediæval glories blend with a host of beautiful items which have been made or procured for it during the past century. Sir Ninian Comper designed the reredos in the south chapel in 1919, and the glass in the window above it. The sanctuary has a long High Altar, adorned with six handsome candlesticks and a grand crucifix. A mighty and magnificent lamp burns before the Blessed Sacrament in the aumbry to the north, and reproduction mediæval glass (the originals are at All Souls College, Oxford) was placed in the east window in 1973. The statues, shrines and aids to devotion here are all so worthy and (with the possible exception of the unusual Stations of the Cross) they blend so well with the work of past ages for which Ufford is so justly famous.

There was already a weekly celebration of the Holy Communion when the Rev'd Hubert Delaval Astley (1891-5) arrived here from the Christ Church Oxford Mission Church of St Frideswide, Poplar in London's East End. During his short ministry here the church and its services underwent a transformation. New altar hangings and frontals; the Italian candlesticks were installed in 1891-2, the box-pews were removed in 1893, a new oak pulpit was given in 1894 by the poor of the parish, and the Continental Stations of the Cross and the pulpit crucifix (1894) were presented by Fr Astley's friend, the Duchess of Santo Teodoro, who resided at Naples. These were five years of careful and intense teaching which established a tradition that has lasted. Here Fr Astley was considerably helped by visits from the Adderley brothers – The Rev'd, the Hon James Adderley (who had worked with him at St Frideswide) and the Rev'd the Hon Richard Adderley (Vicar of Chesterfield), who conducted two Missions here. By the time that Fr Astley left to be Vicar of Ellesborough (the parish church for Chequers), Ufford had a weekly Sung Eucharist, wafer bread and Eucharistic vestments firmly established.

Fr Herbert Williams (1895-1903) arrived here from a curacy at the extreme church of St Matthias, Earls Court and under him Ufford advanced to become a very lively centre of Catholic worship. He immediately began a daily celebration of the Mass, and the use of incense, and gradually established a variety of services, including a Procession of Palms and a Rogation Procession. During his time here a new organ was erected above the rood beam in front of the chancel arch, a new High Altar was installed, with a dossal curtain, which blocked part of the east window behind it, and the tower screen was made to the designs of Mr Leonard Martin. In 1896, a small Mission Church of the Good Shepherd was opened in Upper Ufford and a cottage nearby fitted out for a curate to live in. That year, the parishioners were given a mild telling off in the

The Interior before the removal of the organ to the west end in 1911.

The High Altar before the removal of the Dossal Curtain in 1967.

parish magazine because so few of them celebrated Ascension Day properly by availing themselves of the 4.45 am Eucharist! In November 1896 another Mission was held in the parish, this time conducted by Fr William Black whose father and sister came to live at Ufford. A Stonemasons' Guild was formed and in 1897 these people produced the carved decoration surrounding the main entrance.

There was some opposition during Fr Williams' time here and when in 1897 'a Protestant Lecturer of the Kensit type' came to the Wesleyan Chapel, the Rector invited him to make the Rectory his home during his stay but not surprisingly the offer was declined. Fr Williams did admit that 'in the Rector's wicked heart there lurked a desire to see the instruments of torture purported to be used in the monasteries that the Lecturer carried with him'! Another Protestant Lecturer tried to prevent a girl from making her confession at Ufford by saying that the Rector had related the details of another girl's confession in the village inn. A later visit by Protestant Street Preachers was commented on by Fr Williams who said that they were welcome in the village because they made people think.

Fr Williams and his curate worked hard in the parish and the Holy Week and Easter services for 1899 show how busy the church of a small village had become. On Good Friday of that year there were no less than eight services, including the Three Hours Devotion, the Disbanding of the Lenten Guild and Tenebrae. Four services took place on Holy Saturday and on the Sunday, in addition to Matins, Children's Service and Evensong, there were Masses at 5.00 am (18 communicants), 6.00 am (20 communicants), 7.00 am (55 communicants), 8.00 am (19 communicants) and Solemn Mass at 11.00 am (13 communicants).

Fr Williams exchanged livings with Fr A. S. Hewlett of St John, Horsleydown, London who was in turn succeeded in 1907 by Fr Walter Wyon from St Issey, Cornwall. He had made a hanging pyx for Mr Athelston Riley's neighbouring church of Little Petherick, in whose churchyard he was laid to rest in 1929. The organ was moved from its lofty position above the rood beam in 1911 and was rebuilt at the west end of the nave.

In 1919, Fr Herbert Drake began his long ministry here, which lasted until 1948. Under him the Mass of the Presanctified enriched the worship on Good Friday and the Easter Ceremonies on Holy Saturday. It is interesting to note in the service register, beside the early Mass on a day in September 1943, the signature of Sandys Wason, the exiled priest of Cury with Gunwalloe.

WOODBRIDGE – *School Chapel of St Mary and St Francis*

There was a school in existence before the present one was refounded in 1662 and the buildings that we see today are situated in attractive and extensive undulating grounds. During the Head Mastership of Canon Dudley Symon (1921-47), the School developed a decidedly Catholic tradition, which we may still detect in its attractive and distinctive chapel, which was dedicated in 1927. The building was designed by F. C. Eden and was erected mainly by people in the school, under the direction of the school carpenter. It is an unusual building, its exterior looking somewhat like a little Colonial church with weatherboarded walls and a pantiled roof. Its western entrance is beneath a portico which is supported upon four tapering wooden pillars. Its interior is bright and homely – simple and almost rustic – but not lacking in dignity. The High Altar has a mensa slab of black Belgian marble, a tabernacle and six 17th century Italian candlesticks.

The Chapel was dedicated by the Right Rev'd Arthur Chandler, formerly Bishop of Bloemfontein, and from the beginning there was a Sung Mass every Sunday, a daily celebration, Reservation of the Sacrament and confessions. During Canon Symon's Head Mastership several well-known figures in the

Catholic Movement preached here, including Fr Hampden Thompson of St Mary, Somers Town and Fr Desmond Morse-Boycott, who always took a keen interest in the school; several of his lads from St Mary of the Angels Choir School won scholarships here. Fr F. G. Baring (Chaplain 1928-31) worked in at least eleven Public Schools (including St Michael's, Otford, founded by Fr Tooth) and had been Chaplain of Chichester Theological College. He wrote a book entitled *The Catholic Faith in Public Schools*. His successor, Fr G. H. Stevens, came from a curacy at St Barnabas, Pimlico. Under later chaplains, although it has fluctuated somewhat, the sacramental tradition, which Dudley Symon implanted here, has "stuck".

WOOLVERSTONE – *St Michael and All Angels*

A picturesque church in a lovely parkland setting, across from Woolverstone Hall, the former home of the Berners family and now a school. The Berners have lavished much upon this building, which was once a small church, but has been greatly enlarged. An avenue of clipped yews leads up to the Tudor brick and timber porch. The mediæval church (restored by George Gilbert Scott in 1862) now forms the south aisle for a handsome nave, chancel and grand northern vestry, built in 1888 to the designs of St Aubyn and Wadling through the generosity of Captain Berners.

Inside, St Michael's still has a 19th-century High Church feel, which is enhanced by the richly embroidered banner of St Michael and his large statue in the south aisle, the huge standing coronas each with seven candles, the gentle rise of seven steps from the nave to the High Altar and the multi-coloured tiles in the floors of the chancel and sanctuary. The woodwork of the roofs came from trees grown on the estate. The stately canopied stone sedilia and piscina, together with much of the wood and stone carving, is the work of Thomas Earp.

The six candlesticks given in 1896 for the High Altar are not now in regular use. They have tall wooden stocks which are illuminated with coloured designs and have metal clasps with "IHS" shields at the junction where the real candles fitted. The sanctuary lamp and altar crucifix are also in safekeeping.

Woolverstone was quite a sentinel of the Catholic Movement at the end of the nineteenth century. The Rector (Frederick Wood, 1869-1919) lived at Erwarton, and Curates-in-Charge cared for Woolverstone. The Rev'd T. Earnshaw (1875-88) left to become Vicar of St Faith, Wandsworth. The Rev'd C. Gregory (1889-93) came here from a curacy at St Barnabas, Pimlico. He was known to use wafer bread and veils for the cross during Lent – so things by then were well advanced. Fr Charles Wakefield, formerly Archdeacon of Nassau, who established the daily Eucharist and a monthly choral Eucharist, succeeded him in 1893, and organised several Retreats at Woolverstone Park. When he left in 1895, he expressed the hope that his successor would make it his aim to establish here the use of incense, plainsong, the Angelus, a monthly Requiem and a weekly Sung Mass. Fr Stowell Jackson (1896-9 and formerly curate of St Martin, Brighton) certainly tried to advance the worship here; he presented candlesticks and a set of processional torches to the church and instituted Solemn Evensong at festivals. His attempt in 1898 to begin a weekly Sung Mass was not successful however. He records in the register 'Churchwarden absent, no-one collected offertory, Low celebration only as choir left church after Morning Prayer'! Fr F. W. Doxat (1899-1903) was also Ward Superior of the local branch of the Confraternity of the Blessed Sacrament; he left to become Vicar of Madingley, Cambridgeshire.

Under the Rev'd J. Utten Todd (Curate-in-Charge, 1903-19 and then Rector until 1949), Woolverstone's worship was somewhat modified, although it continued to be rather "High" by comparison with the surrounding parishes. In the 1890s, however, this parkland church was a leading light in the Catholic Movement in East Suffolk. People came from all over the diocese to the Retreats held in the park and even Fr Cobbold of St Bartholomew, Ipswich wrote in his parish magazine, 'A comparison of Woolverstone vestments with our own resulted somewhat, it must be admitted, in the disparagement of the latter'.

Chapter Three

Brief notes on other Suffolk Churches associated with the Movement and some of their clergy

THESE NOTES are by no means comprehensive but present a selection of churches that the Movement has touched at some time, together with a few of the Clergy who developed a Catholic Tradition in them.

ALPHETON – *St Peter and St Paul*

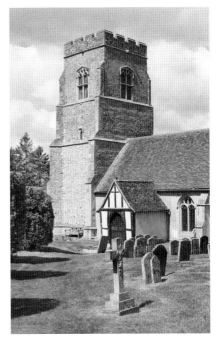

An atmospheric church in a charming and isolated setting, it was restored by the Rev'd Ernest Geldart between 1902 and 1903 and he equipped it with a new priest's stall, altar and reredos. The Patron of the livings of Shimplingthorne and Alpheton during the ministry of the Rev'd Joseph Williamson was Fr W. F. Buttle of St Chad's, Haggerston. 'Father Joe' – later to be known for his work amongst prostitutes in London's East End – worked hard to restore this church during his time here, approaching many famous people (including members of the Royal Family) for help – and getting it!

Henry Hooke Bartrum (1901-16) – Author of *Sermons on the Black Letter Saints.*

Joseph Williamson (1934-49) – Curate of Ss Michael and George, Fulwell and St James, Norlands, Kensington. Later Vicar of St Paul, Dock Street. Author of *Father Joe* and *Friends of Father Joe.*

Fr Joseph Williamson.

Guy E. J. Moss (1951-5) – Curate of St Chrysostom, Peckham and St Nicholas, Guildford. Later Chaplain and Sub-Warden to the Community of All Hallows, Ditchingham.

BLUNDESTON – *St Mary*

A Lothingland church with a picturesque round tower, broad, lofty nave and much Victorian woodwork, with a well-appointed English altar (*c.*1928) and several statues, including Our Lady of Walsingham.

B. D. Godfrey (1935-45) – Vestments, sanctuary lamp, Missal and altar hangings given during his time.

C. H. Hubbins (1945-74) – Introduced a daily Mass and links with Walsingham.

BRAISEWORTH – *St Mary*

This is a distinctive pseudo-Norman church (1857) by Edward Buckton Lamb, incorporating mediæval work from the old church. It is now beautifully converted into a house.

Thomas Holt Wilson (1904-7) – Weekly Communion.

Herbert Drake (1907-19) – Sung Eucharist every Sunday. St Christopher's Home for Boys opened in 1915. A book about Suffolk written in 1908 mentions an old and valuable chasuble of silver fabric, enriched with heavy gilt embroidery, formerly in use at a nunnery and presented to the church by the Rev'd T. C. Elsdon, where it continued to be used. From 1919 the parish was linked with Eye.

BURES – *St Mary*

This lovely and welcoming church, fascinating outside and in, has been tastefully re-ordered and has many signs that it is very much alive. It has changed somewhat since the time of the clergy with birettas whose photographs in the vestry remind us of its Anglo-

Catholic past. The sanctuary lamp still hangs before the High Altar and when I visited in 1988 the disused tabernacle still occupied the niche in the Waldegrave Chapel. Then hidden by a curtain, 1920s paintings of a Host in the monstrance, flanked by angels with candles and censers and two Saints, occupied the panels of the late 19th-century reredos, with its marble gradine. Now only the Angel Gabriel and the Blessed Virgin Mary remain at each end. The Waldegrave Chapel was restored for its proper use in 1927. Christ the King looks out from its east window in glass of 1940 by Horace Wilkinson, which bids us pray for the chapel's 16th-century builders and for their descendants.

W. H. E. R. Jervis (1888-1907) – Vicar of St Paul, Colchester and Cranford, Middlesex. Editor of the Gregorian Psalter.

J. E. Varley (1911-6) – Curate of Holy Trinity, Frome and St Gregory, Canterbury. Rector of Ilmer, Bucks. Exchanged livings with Fr Molesworth.

E. H. Molesworth (1916-23) – Curate of St James, Norlands, Kensington and Christ Church, Paddington. Rector of Jedburgh, St George, Edinburgh, St Philip, Maidstone, Clapham and Patching, Sussex and then of Bures.

J. W. Green (1923-39) – Curate of St Mary, Woolwich, St Stephen, Lewisham, and East Ham. Vicar at St Edmund, Forest Gate, St Anne, Limehouse and Bures.

N. G. Stephenson (1939-49) – Curate of St Stephen, Upton Park, Woodbridge, St Thomas, Ipswich and St Alban, Upton Park. Curate-in-Charge of St Martin, Plaistow and Vicar at Bures.

C. H. Sharp (1949-56) – Formerly Curate-in-Charge of St Stephen, Colchester.

Michael C. Brown (1956-62) – Curate of St Michael, Mill Hill and St Paul, Knightsbridge. Left to become Rector of Godalming, Surrey.

Ian Dunlop (1962-72) – Left to become Canon Chancellor of Salisbury Cathedral.

CAVENDISH – *St Mary*

A great feature in this church, which is full of treasures, is a stunning reredos, now in the north aisle, which is 16th-century Flemish work, with surrounds by Sir Ninian Comper. This was the property of the prominent Anglo-Catholic layman, Mr Athelston Riley and came from his private chapel in London. His daughter, Mrs Morwenna Brocklebank, presented it to Cavendish in 1950.

Robert G. Peter (1860-95) – Formerly Tutor at Jesus College, Oxford.

R. Wilson (1895-1908) – Formerly Vicar of Guilden Morden.

W. K. Lowther Clarke (1908-15) – Formerly Curate of St Matthew, Moorfields, Bristol and Rector of Harlton, Cambridgeshire.

Detail from 16th-century reredos.

J. D. Barnard (1915-63) – Canon Barnard was Curate at St Clement, York, then, after a brief period abroad, came to Cavendish where he remained for 48 years.

GREAT CORNARD – *St Andrew*

A picturesque exterior, with a distinctive shingled spire and a Tudor brick staircase turret. The interior has been greatly restored but is attractive and some of its Anglo-Catholic fittings remain.

A. H. Sellwood (1929-35) – He introduced Sung Mass every Sunday and also Reservation. Incense was used here first in 1931. On Easter Day the Sung Mass was often accompanied by organ, orchestra and augmented choir, who rendered Handel's Halleluiah Chorus! He wrote in the register before he left, 'Thanks be to God for a most happy ministry with these dear people of Cornard'.

The High Altar.

The Chancel at Great Cornard where Fr Sellwood's "dear people" worshipped.

GREAT FINBOROUGH – *St Andrew*

Richard M. Phipson's hilltop masterpiece of 1874 to 1877 has a resplendent exterior in flint and stone and its glorious spire is visible for miles. The lofty and dignified interior, rich in Clayton & Bell glass, has Victorian radiators protected by iron openwork fronts and marble shelves above! The north transept, originally for the Manor family with memorials (several from the old church) to the Wollastons and the Pettiwards, later became the Lady Chapel and its little English altar is still here. The First World War memorial rood screen with rood group announces "Jesu, Mercy". The sanctuary lamps, sets of vestments (including black) and thurible remain from its Anglo-Catholic heyday in the 1920s and 1930s.

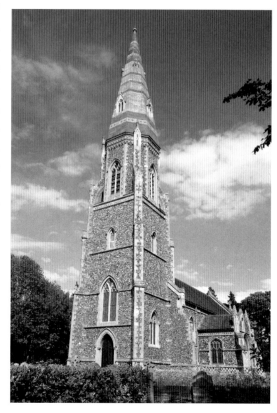

Thomas Housecroft (1900-10) – Vicar of Wickham Market. Rector of Woodbridge. Instituted weekly communions by 1902.

Fennel Fitzpatrick (1910-28) – Became a Forces Chaplain in World War I and Fr R. H. Nottage, who was in charge here from 1917 to 1920 introduced daily mass and Sung Mass every Sunday, Vespers of the Blessed Sacrament at *Corpus Christi* and Devotions as part of the Peace Thanksgiving. On his return the Vicar continued the daily Eucharist and weekly Sung Eucharist.

Charles Fisher (1928-36) – Exchanged the living of St Margaret, Burnley with Fr Fitzpatrick, having previously been Curate at Chesterfield. He maintained a fairly advanced tradition here, with Low Mass and Sung Mass each Sunday. Mr Kensit's Wickliffe Preachers 'witnessed mass' here in 1931 and held a protest meeting afterwards, followed by an address in the Congregational Chapel to enlighten the parishioners further concerning 'Father Fisher's practices'.

HUNDON – *All Saints*

This church, with its fine setting and stately exterior, was reduced to a shell by fire in 1914 and was rebuilt to the designs of Mr Detmar Blow. Its interior is spacious and bright – attractive and very devotional. It is, however, very simple and homely and shows what the right use of space and colour can create. The long High Altar of stone has simple ornaments and frontals in subdued colours. Equally simple is the Requiem Chapel in the north aisle. Steps descend to the Lady Chapel where the Blessed Sacrament is reserved. All is functional and unprepossessing, yet dignified and tasteful. One can feel that this building has been much prayed in.

Henry F. Gipps (1896-1914) – The Holy Eucharist established as the main service on Sundays and Saints Days. A Mission was held here in 1901 by the Society of the Resurrection.

John H. Burn (1914-9) – Church destroyed by fire in 1914. Re-opened in 1916.

M. W. Champneys (1920-9) – Curate of Little St Mary, Cambridge and the Annunciation, St Marylebone. Regular Choral Eucharist here. Also several regular weekday masses and Midnight Mass at Christmas.

A. F. Waskett (1929-81) – This saintly and hardworking priest loved, served and prayed for the people of Hundon for 52 years, maintaining the Catholic tradition here with daily Mass, Reservation, incense, etc. It was the influence of Army Chaplains during the First World War that led him to study for ordination and he arrived at Hundon a young widower with two small children. Fr Waskett was a man of prayer and his intercession for people gained him a remarkable reputation for healing the sick, which brought him requests for prayer from people all over the world. He was also widely sought as a confessor and spiritual director. He was made an Honorary Canon of the Cathedral in 1973 and during the late seventies he published three books of meditations. A fractured hip caused him to resign in 1981 at the age of 91 and he died in the November of that year.

Fr Waskett.

IPSWICH – *All Saints*

James Brooks' entry in the competition for a design for All Saints, Ipswich; the realisation of the winning design is shown on facing page.

An architectural competition for the design of All Saints was won by Samuel Wright of Morecambe, who in 1887, provided the fine brick and terracotta church, distinguished by its tall and eccentric octagonal tower.

Caesar Caine (1901-10) – Fr Williams of Ufford wrote of Fr Caine: 'he was, until a few years ago, a Wesleyan, but through study was led to accept the Catholic Faith in its entirety'. This energetic and hardworking Priest laid the foundations of the Catholic tradition in this parish. The Easter Sunday before his departure saw six celebrations of the Eucharist and a total of 526 communicants.

S. W. Key (1910-25) – Formerly Curate of Chislehurst. During his time All Saints was noted for its processions, which were the first outdoor processions in Ipswich since the Reformation. Some 700 people took part in the All Saints Tide procession in 1913.

S. C. Calver (1925-36) – Trained at St John, Felixstowe. During his time Fr Colin Gill (later of St Magnus the Martyr, London and Master of the Guardians of the Shrine at Walsingham) served a curacy here.

IPSWICH – *St Thomas*

St Thomas began life as a daughter church of All Saints. A 'tin tabernacle' designed by Raymond Wrinch, was erected in Bramford Road in 1902, during Fr Caesar Caine's ministry at All Saints. It was beautifully furnished with full sets of altar frontals, a simple chancel screen, choir stalls from Bramford church and six tall candles. The present church is a distinctive building of 1937 by N. F. Cachemaille-Day with a fine 60-foot tower. A colourful and devotional interior with a long High Altar, an impressive modern aumbry in the north chapel and Stations of the Cross by the

Benedictine Nuns at Cockfosters. Curates in Charge and Vicars have included:

The Interior of the 'Tin Tabernacle' predecessor to the present building by Cachemaille-Day.

C. R. Phillips (1911-26) – Formerly Curate of St John, Longton, Staffordshire.

D. E. Rae (1927-31) – Later Vicar of St Giles, Norwich.

T. G. Davies (1949-57) – Later Archdeacon of Lewisham.

K. W. Brassell (1957-62) – Later Vicar of St James, Elmer's End, Beckenham.

D. C. Gooderham (1961-4) – Later Vicar of St Bartholomew, Ipswich.

R. G. Ball (1964-81) – Was Curate at St Barnabas, Northolt and St Etheldreda, Fulham.

KEDINGTON – *St Peter and St Paul*

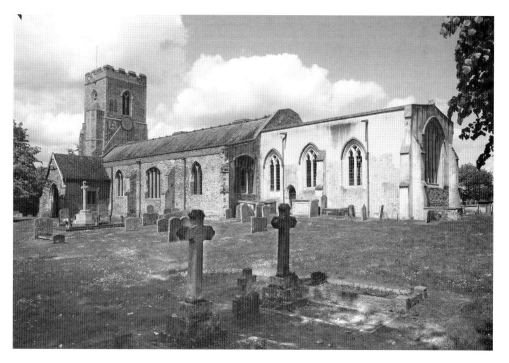

This church, sometimes known as the "Westminster Abbey of Suffolk", is of tremendous interest for its fittings and superb monuments. A sensitive restoration by William Weir (1931) has preserved the character of a church that was almost untouched by the Victorians. Very awkward to make the best use of liturgically, but liberal Catholic worship continues here. The patrons are the Walsingham College Trust.

George Perry (1910-29) – Holy Communion on Sunday and Saints days and a monthly Choral Celebration. Crucifix erected over the chancel screen in 1926.

The Interior looking east from the Musician's Gallery.

William Turnbull (1929-53) – Monthly Sung Eucharist. Chapel at the east end of the north aisle.

J. C. Ryder (1953-9) – Sung Mass every Sunday. Walsingham Children's Home supported.

Peter Harbottle (1959-64) – Daily Mass. Links with Walsingham strengthened. Reservation 1960. Fr Harbottle had been a Lay Brother in Fr Hope Patten's Community of St Augustine at Walsingham from 1936 to 1950. After ordination he worked in the West Indies. He returned to become Curate of St Paul, Chiswick, then of Walsingham, before coming to Kedington. He left to be Vicar of St Michael, Edmonton.

William Mason (1972-87) – Had been a Shrine Priest at Walsingham. Celebrated patronal festivals with Sung Mass in the morning and events in the afternoon culminating in strawberry tea and Benediction.

LAKENHEATH – *St Mary*

This church, in the far northwest of the county, between the Fens and Thetford Forest, is a treasure house for the church enthusiast, with its Norman chancel arch, its fine roofs, exquisite benches, wall paintings, rare mediæval pulpit, and much else. Set in a feast of antiquity, its atmosphere enhanced by largely unrenewed floors, are colourful and devotional furnishings that are the product of its Catholic tradition. Many of these date from the second half of the 20th century, including the colourful reversible nave altar and the beautiful font cover, both the work of Siegfried Pietzsch. The crucifix over the High Altar was painted by Mark Cazalet and fashioned in bog-oak by local craftsman, William Horrex. Fr James Mather (1995-2001) equipped the High Altar with six candlesticks and a tabernacle. The statue of Our Lady, which occupies a mediæval recess near the entrance, was brought here from Eye parish church in 1974.

Frederick Charles Scrivener (1874-1902) – Arrived here from a curacy at Guiting Power where, some 20 years later, Fr Aelred Carlyle and his Benedictine monks were to set up their monastery for a brief six-month stay.

John G. M. Stretton (1902-19) – His curacies included St Olave, Exeter, St Cyprian, Clarence Gate, All Souls, Harlesden and St John, Walworth. He was Curate-in-Charge of West Row from 1895 to 1902. He established Holy Communion every Sunday, although at the beginning it was often Ante-Communion because nobody turned up. In fact, there were only 21 communicants on Easter Sunday in 1903.

The High Altar today.

Isaac Morris (1919-39) – Fr Morris came here from curacies at St Mary, Stoke, Ipswich and Holy Trinity, Ely and it was he who established a weekly Choral Eucharist and by 1923 the Eucharist was celebrated daily. The church was re-ordered in 1926 when the organ was moved to the west end, the east end of the north aisle was made into a chapel using a redundant altar from St Bartholomew, Ipswich and an aumbry for the reservation of the Blessed Sacrament was made in the north chancel wall. By the time Fr Morris left for St Mary, Newmarket, Catholic Anglicanism was well established in Lakenheath.

Norman E. Marshall (1939-53) had spent most of his ministry in India.

William Edgar Beale (1953-6) later became Rector of Kedington.

Thomas Bernard Beal (1956-63) had been trained at St Alban, Hull and had been Vicar of Bramford and Burstall.

Canon W. A. C. Ullathorne (1964-75) – He ended his full-time ministry here, having served at St John, Bury St Edmunds and St Bartholomew, Ipswich.

MENDHAM – *All Saints*

This is a pretty church set in a lovely village beside the River Waveney. The Parish is in the Patronage of the Guild of All Souls and is now linked with four other parishes. It was a thriving beacon of advanced worship in the late 19th and early 20th centuries.

Newton C. Bennett (1890-2) – Curacies included St Ives, Cornwall and St Matthew, Bethnal Green. After Mendham he was incumbent of St Alban, Fulham, St Martin, Roath and St Luke, Cambridge.

William H. Harris (1892-1906) – Curacies included St Peter, Plymouth and Swanmore, Isle of Wight.

Reginald Egremont (1906-25) – Curate of St Martin, Brighton.

Joseph Vincent (1925-7) – Left to be Vicar of Eye.

Herbert Pitts (1927-9) – Curate of St Alban, Teddington. Left to be Vicar of St James, Norwich.

C. R. Scholes (1929-45) – Curate of St Edmund, Forest Gate and St Edmund, Hunstanton.

Martin Lewis (1953-68) – Curate of St Columba, Haggerston and St Andrew, Worthing.

NAYLAND – *St James*

Set in a peaceful and picturesque corner of a village of ancient houses on the banks of the River Stour. The interior is light, airy and spacious, the nave and chancel being set beneath one continuous 15th-century roof. A Constable painting forms the altarpiece here. Of special note is the more recent work, particularly the north chapel of St Francis, with a memorial window to the Rev'd Gilbert Warwick (died 1960) on the theme of the Blessed Sacrament, and Anton Wagner's (1974) statue of Our Lady of Walsingham in the Lady Chapel.

J. D. Gray (1879-1909) – Holy Communion on Sundays and Saints Days. Choral celebrations on festivals. Vestments worn, for the first time since the Reformation, in 1894.

W. T. Farmiloe (1909-14) – Came from work in the parishes of St Peter, Great Windmill Street and St Augustine, South Hackney. Later Archdeacon of Sudbury and Chaplain of All Saints, Rome.

J. R. Sankey (1915-7) – Curate of St Andrew, Plaistow and St Mary Magdalene, Paddington. He immediately began a Daily Mass here. In 1916 there was a Mission in the parish conducted by Fr T. Preedy. He left Nayland to be Rector of St Andrew by the Wardrobe in the City of London.

J. B. Marsh (1917-23) – Holy Eucharist almost every day and Sung Eucharist every Sunday. A moderate Catholic tradition has continued here ever since.

The fifth Station of the Cross.

ORFORD – *St Bartholomew*

Tall 14th-century nave and aisles and the ruins of a Norman chancel. A good restoration here by J. T. Micklethwaite (1897-1900). The noble and lofty interior is dominated by the magnificent screen (crowned by the rood group), carved by Lawrence Turner to the designs of Sidney Tugwell of Bournemouth. The High Altar retains its 19th-century cross and candlesticks.

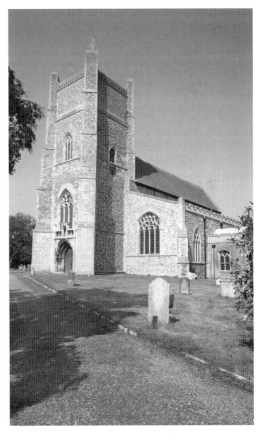

Edward Maude Scott (1877-1901) – He came here from a curacy at St Mary Redcliffe, Bristol at the age of 27. A scholarly Prayer Book Catholic, he transformed the interior into a dignified and devotional setting for worship. According to the *Ritualistic Clergy List* he was a member of the English Church Union.

Frederick Anstruther Cardew (1901-7) – Fr Cardew arrived from the Australian Anglo-Catholic stronghold of All Saints, Brisbane and left to become Chaplain of St George, Paris, where he remained until 1934. There he founded the Theatre Girls' Hostel and it was for his work amongst English girls employed in Paris music halls that he was decorated by the French and British governments.

W. H. E. R. Jervis (1907-14) – (See Bures – p. 96)

H. A. Tudor (1914-35) – He left to become Chaplain of All Saints, Rome.

C. H. K. Sherlock (1956-73) – Had been Vicar of St Gabriel, Bounds Green.

SHOTTISHAM – *St Margaret*

This pretty church, proudly set upon a hill overlooking its village, has an attractive exterior, although both outside and inside there is much work of 1867 to the designs of E. C. Hakewill. The interior has always been simply furnished and the tradition here has never been extreme, but a sound Prayer Book Catholic tradition had become established here by the 1870s with Holy Communion on Sundays and Saints Days and the Offices said daily. For much of the 20th century there has been a Sung Eucharist every Sunday, with the occasional use of incense.

C. F. L. Yonge (1890-1908) – He left to become Rector of Cressing, Essex.

F. J. B. Hart (1908-17) – Later Rector of Kelsale.

A. E. Gledhill (1922-9) – Curate of Hornsey, Horbury and St Paul, Hemel Hempstead. Later Vicar of Holy Trinity, Bungay.

Penrose Berryman (1929-65) – This scholarly priest, who was a Fellow of the Royal Meteorological Society and of the Incorporated Guild of Church Musicians, had been Curate of Barry in Wales and of Bourne Abbey in Lincolnshire.

H. D'Aubri Cullen (1966-86) – Fr Cullen had served his title at the Anglo-Catholic stronghold of St Lawrence, Long Eaton, Derbyshire and came here from St George, Darwen, Lancashire.

SUDBURY – *St Peter*

The church of St Peter has a grand position and a magnificent exterior although it was always a Chapel of Ease to St Gregory. Butterfield restored it between 1854 and 1858, replacing the old box pews with chairs, much to the annoyance of Sudbury folk. G. F. Bodley designed the magnificent reredos, which was erected in 1897. There is fine glass by Hardman of Birmingham and a splendid organ by T. C. Lewis. Now in the care of the Churches Conservation Trust, this splendid church is much loved and greatly used.

J. Henley (1851-5) – Accused of 'correctly tendering the doctrines of the Tractarian School'. He began a daily Choral Service (probably Evensong) here.

The Chancel, showing the censing angels which flanked the Chancel Arch.

J. W. H. Molyneux (1855-79) – Started weekly choral celebrations of the Holy Communion and gave clear and definite Catholic teaching, especially about the priesthood and the sacraments. Preachers here included John Keble and Edward Stuart of St Mary Magdalene, Munster Square.

THELNETHAM – *St Nicholas*

This is an idyllically-set church with beautiful architectural features and tremendous character. In 1895 two mediæval mensa-slabs, one discovered in the church floor and the other in the churchyard, were incorporated by Faculty into new altars in the chancel and Lady Chapel. The rood screen and crucifix (1907) and the Stations of the Cross also remind us of the Catholic tradition which developed here.

Canon J. S. Sawbridge (1871-1925), He succeeded his father as Rector here and remained for an amazing 54 years. He was trained at Cuddesdon under Edward King (later Bishop of Lincoln). It was said of Canon Sawbridge that 'his whole life and pastoral work were embued with the very spirit of Keble, the doctrine of Liddon, the love and spiritual grace of King'. He conserved and beautified the church by spearheading three restoration programmes (1871 to 1872 by R. M. Phipson, 1895 by W. M. Fawcett and 1906 by T. D. Atkinson). A passionate promoter of education, who crusaded for the retention of church schools, he founded St Helen's School at Thelnetham in 1872 and St Mary's School, Coney Weston in 1897. Thelnetham rectory hosted several annual festivals of Church Elementary School Teachers and Sunday School Teachers, and of the Girls' Friendly Society and Missionary Festivals. He was an enthusiastic expert on flowers, trees and birds, who was also experienced in farming, landscape gardening and estate management. Above all he was a wise and caring Tractarian country parish priest.

E. H. Bevan (1925-6) – Formerly Bishop of Southern Rhodesia.

C. E. L. Cowen (1927-36) – Curate of St Paul, Burton on Trent. Spent most of his ministry as a Naval Chaplain. Vicar of St Boniface, Devonport from 1923 to 1926.

W. H. Finlayson (1936-46) – Curate of St John, South Hackney and St John, Holland Road, Kensington. Rector of Letheringsett and later of Framingham Pigot and Framingham Earl, Norfolk.

TRIMLEY – *St Mary*

William Butterfield carried out some restoration work here in 1855 and Fr R. H. Faulconer transformed the interior between 1901 and 1902. Inside, St Mary's is grand, dignified and Tractarian, culminating in a richly furnished chancel with hanging candelabra, panelled wainscoting, large aumbry doors and High Altar set high with richly embroidered frontals and backed by a noble reredos. There is some beautiful glass by Powell, including the face of Bishop King of Lincoln. The many similarities to the work by J. S. Corder, undertaken for Fr Faulconer when he was at Swilland, suggests Corder almost certainly also worked at Trimley.

R. H. Faulconer (1897-1904) – Established Holy Communion every Sunday, Thursday and on Saints days and also a monthly Choral Celebration.

Armine Wodehouse (1904-22) – Had served curacies at St Luke, Maidenhead and St Giles, Reading and came here from the parish of Chelmondiston.

WESTHORPE – *St Margaret*

A charming and unspoilt church, steeped in atmosphere. Its mediæval High Altar mensa was restored to its rightful use in 1912. Fr Wareham adorned the altar with six handsome Baroque style candlesticks. Several items from his time here remain, including the tiny sanctuary lamp in the south chapel entrance, Our Lady's statue, framed articles of Church teaching near the main entrance and some beautiful vestments.

P. T. E. Wareham (1920-32) He was Curate at St Agnes, Kennington Park and at Stanford, Norfolk. He left to become Vicar of Mendlesham. He turned this church into a devotional shrine, making the most of its mediæval treasures and atmosphere. Under him this small parish became a stronghold of Catholic worship.

WICKHAM MARKET – *All Saints*

This hilltop church, with its amazing octagonal tower and tall spire, has been a vibrant centre of Evangelical churchmanship for just over 100 years. Yet the visitor may still see here evidence of its Anglo-Catholic period that lasted from 1869 to 1905. When E. C. Hakewill supervised a thorough restoration of the church in 1869/70, he gave the statue of the Virgin and Child that still adorns the external niche above the west window. One of the special preachers at the re-opening services was Fr A. H. Stanton of St Alban, Holborn. Apostles, Martyrs, Prophets and Latin Doctors look upwards on Michael Buckley's painted reredos of 1881 towards the stone figure of Christ fixed to the east window tracery. Fr W. H. C. Luke of St Matthias, Earls Court preached at the re-opening after this work and the pulpit was occupied after further restoration work in 1892 by Fr Charles Brooke of St John the Divine, Kennington.

William T. Image (1866-89) – A wise and talented Tractarian who gently taught the Faith to Wickham Market people, gaining their respect and affection. He spearheaded the church's restoration according to the principles of the Ecclesiological Movement and developed a fine musical tradition here.

Thomas Housecroft (1889-96) and **Richard Denman-Dean** (1896-9) – Both maintained the tradition and both moved from this parish to become Rector of St Mary, Woodbridge.

Edward H. Griffith (1899-1905) – Came here with very extreme ideas having spent his previous 19 years' ministry serving eight curacies. Not only did he enrage local Protestants, but he also alienated many of his congregation who preferred to worship elsewhere. The service register records only 17 communicants on Easter Day in 1901. His speedy resignation in 1905 was shortly followed by his trial before a Consistory Court for immorality with a lady from Campsea Ash and his subsequent unfrocking. This scandal was the last straw for Wickham Market Anglicans and the patronage of the living was transferred into the Evangelical hands of the Church Trust Fund trustees.

WOODBRIDGE – *St Mary*

The interior of this splendid 15th-century town church was transformed by R. M. Phipson between 1874 and 1875 and was again beautified between 1935 and 1948 to the designs of W. A. Forsyth, whose work included the font cover, reredos and what was an English High Altar with an aumbry behind it (the aumbry was moved northwards in 1952). The striking glass in the east window (dedicated in 1946) is by Martin Travers. An ambitious 21st-century re-ordering has created a new nave altar and choir stalls and the transformation of the area of the base of the tower.

R. C. M. Rouse (1870-87) – Established Holy Communion every Sunday, services on Saints days and a robed choir, but always maintained his 'thorough loyalty to the Reformed Church'.

Thomas Housecroft (1896-9) – He came here from Wickham Market and left to be Rector of Great Finborough and later of Limpenhoe, Norfolk.

R. Denman Dean (1900-15) – Saints days kept and monthly Choral celebrations of the Holy Communion. Much Catholic teaching given and many guest preachers from more advanced parishes in the diocese. The Sanctus bell was rung for the first time in 1912. Vestments and possibly incense were introduced during his time.

Robert B. Dand (1927-48) – Curate at St Clement, Notting Dale and St Vedast, Foster Lane, London. By this time there was Choral Eucharist every Sunday, Reservation in an aumbry behind the High Altar, daily Eucharist and incense. Great celebrations in 1933 for the centenary of the Oxford Movement, although in the parish magazine Fr Dand was very scathing about 'extremists, who would be better in Rome'.

WORTHAM – *St Mary*

This fine church has the shell of England's largest round tower and is still furnished with its three altars, several crucifixes and a small statue of Our Lady of Walsingham, although its present tradition is more central.

J. F. E. Faning (1903-25) – Former Chaplain of King's College, Cambridge (Wortham's Patrons). Holy Communion on Sundays and Saints days. UMCA and SPG supported.

F. C. Moore (1925-35) – He established a definite Catholic tradition, with Low Mass on Sundays and Saints days, Sung Mass on alternate Sundays, special Holy Week services, Requiem masses, etc. He also had links with the Shrine of Our Lady at Walsingham.

H. G. Hiller (1935-59) – Former King's Choral Scholar and Precentor of Norwich Cathedral. He instituted a children's Eucharist and the Litany sung in procession at Rogationtide.

YAXLEY – *St Mary*

A beautiful church with a splendid 15th-century porch, roof and screen.

W. H. Sewell (1861-97) – A noted naturalist, historian and moderate Catholic. He left his private Communion set for the sick, which included a stone altar-slab and leather-covered pyx, to the church.

G. B. Nash (1897-1924) He wore vestments and also steered a moderate Catholic course.

R. C. Magee (1924-49) – Curate at St Barnabas, Pimlico. Fr Colin Gill conducted a Mission here in 1930.

Chapter Four

Some notable clergy

THE FOLLOWING CHARACTERS form but a small selection from a multitude of clergy who, over the past 150 years, have to a greater or lesser extent fostered the Catholic tradition in Suffolk parishes. There were so many who, in times when such things were rare, encouraged their people to see the English Church as a part of the Church Catholic and its priesthood as part of the heritage passed down from Christ Himself through the Apostolic Succession, and who made their churches beautiful and dignified places of sacramental worship and nourished their people with the sacraments and with sound teaching. There were many priests who taught the Faith, even if some of the "trimmings" were absent, and so played their part in bringing back to the Church of England a realisation of its Catholic heritage. In years gone by, of course, there was no idea of the principle of the shared ministry and we must remember that it was very much the personality and convictions of the parish priest that steered the life of the parish church. He did the thinking, the teaching, the counselling, and much of the rest of the work which made the parish tick – on his own.

GEORGE DRURY – *Claydon*

One of the most controversial figures of the Movement in the 19th century was the Rev'd George Drury, Rector of Claydon and Akenham from 1846 to 1895. The living belonged to his family and he, in turn, was both Rector and Patron. He embraced the principles of the Oxford Movement very early on and he furnished Claydon Church in line with its ideals. Spurred on by his keenness to see the monastic life revived in the Church of England, he gave hospitality to Joseph Leycester Lyne (Fr Ignatius OSB) and his handful of monks, who made their home at Claydon Rectory and who assisted in the parish from Shrove Tuesday 1863 until January 1864.

Ignatius (who remained in deacon's orders for most of his life) was one of the most dynamic and determined eccentrics that the Church of England has ever produced. His driving aim was to revive Benedictine monasticism on the most lavish and the most severe lines. He combined riveting evangelical hell-fire preaching with the most extreme Continental ceremonial. Suffolk folk had never seen anything like it in their lives and in his few brief months at Claydon the young monk stirred up a hornet's nest! Local and national newspapers broadcast the stories of the goings-on in this quiet Suffolk village. Ignatius converted many people, but many more were determined to rid Suffolk of the monk and of the popish priest who had entertained him.

Although the *outré* and unashamed ceremonial which Ignatius brought to Claydon found a delighted and willing protagonist in Fr Drury, the incidents of 1863 and 1864 were to blacken his name in many places for the rest of his life. This was a pity because it is clear that he was a prayerful and conscientious priest, who worked hard and had built up a committed and Catholic minded congregation without the influence of Ignatius.

In the days when few clergy did so, Fr Drury walked about his parish dressed in cassock and biretta and unashamedly used full Catholic ceremonial, including incense, in his church. An idea of the celebrations at Claydon during the period when Ignatius was assisting him may be seen from accounts of what took place on Ascension Day and St Peter's Day 1863. On each occasion the evening preceding the festival saw a solemn procession from the Rectory to a full church for a Vigil service; then on the day itself a Low Mass at 8.30 am, Morning Prayer at 10.00 am, a full Solemn Mass at 11.00 am, and Solemn Evensong with Procession at 7.00 pm. The St Peter's Day Mass included the Kyrie from Mendelssohn's Elijah and the Sanctus and Gloria from Mozart's Second and Twelfth masses. The evening procession, with acolytes, thurifer, servers, choristers, monks and at least four banners, wound its way through the streets of Claydon, headed by the crucifix, before returning to a church bedecked in cloth of silver on its east wall, a cloth of gold altar frontal and the cross and candlesticks upon the reredos wreathed in summer flowers. Such awful disturbances followed this procession that Ignatius was prevented from giving his prepared lecture about St Peter. His hood was wrenched from his head and a drunken 'Protestant', having threatened Ignatius and Drury with a large stick, accidentally struck the churchwarden's little son to the ground with a violent blow to the head. On Ascension Eve, Ignatius preached (this was just before Bishop Pelham inhibited him from doing so) but the sermon had to stop because Drury spotted a reporter in the congregation and went down to have a stand-up argument with him.

The newspaper report of a First Communion service says, 'To what are we coming when children of the tender age of twelve receive the Sacrament?' At this 8.00 am celebration, twenty newly-confirmed children assembled at the convent in the village and processed to a packed church, the girls wearing white veils and carrying bouquets of roses. Shortly after Ignatius left for Norwich, Fr Drury set up a Benedictine convent for women in a large house in the village street, owned by a Miss Ware; this lasted until 1882.

Fr Drury was a man of considerable artistic talent. He designed and made the stained glass in Claydon's east window, including a representation of Our Lady of Walsingham long before the Shrine's revival. The refurbishing of the chancel, the tower pinnacles and the intricately traceried pulpit were largely his inspiration. He built the strange flint walls and mock ruins in his Rectory garden, probably with masonry from the ruined church at Thurleston. He made bricks in a kiln in the Rectory precincts.

He was the subject of rudeness and ridicule for much of his ministry. It flared up again in 1878 during the Akenham Burial Case. His Bishop censured him twice and his nine-foot high Rectory wall saved him and his family from much violence, yet when he died in 1895, the newspapers had to admit that 'only an undoubtedly sincere man would have stood the test from which he did not shrink'.

JOHN W. H. MOLYNEUX – *St Gregory and St Peter, Sudbury.*

It was said of the Rev'd Sir John Molyneux, Bt, that he was 'next to Mr Drury the most notorious man in the county for his Puseyism'. He received a fine training for this at St Mary Magdalene, Munster Square, St Marylebone and his forthright teaching about the Holy Eucharist, the Real Presence of Jesus in the Sacrament and the sacrificial nature of the priesthood brought about a storm of abuse. One of his churchwardens wrote in 1858 that within weeks of his arrival he was pulling down galleries and pews in the church, had re-introduced 'full choral services', had erected a super-altar on the Communion table and had placed candlesticks with candles there, together with a large cross on the altar and little ornamental ones in various parts of the church. Newspapers were reporting his intoning in Latin, his genuflexions and use of the eastward position at the altar. The question of lighted candles led to a long correspondence between Molyneux and Bishop Browne of Ely in 1865, with the former resolutely defending their use.

He hated the pew system and abolished it in his churches, removing the galleries and the box pews and selling the timber on the Market Hill. He furnished the churches with rush-bottomed chairs which were entirely free of pew-rents, making clear in a letter to the parishioners that 'Earthly distinctions have no place in the house of God' and describing the reservation and renting of seats in church as 'a striking manifestation of the power of the Devil and his agents'.

His ceremonial, however, was nowhere near as advanced as Drury's. A newspaper correspondent in 1864, signing himself *Anglicanus Catholicus,* and referring to the disagreement in Sudbury between 'the miserable bigoted sectarian Protestantism of Dissenters and Low Church schismatics and the revived Catholic usages of the Anglican Church' commended him for what he had already achieved, but regretted that 'despite Mr Molyneux's advanced views, processions, Mass vestments, incense, etc.' had not been introduced in his churches.

He was Rector of St Gregory and St Peter, Sudbury from 1855 until 1879 and inherited his baronetcy two months before he died. Bishop Woodford made him a Canon of Ely Cathedral in 1875. His obituary in 1879 states that although he had 'High Church views', as soon as it was declared illegal to have lighted candles on the altar he discontinued their use, leaving the candlesticks in place. An active opponent of vivisection, he helped with the formation of the Sudbury branch of the RSPCA.

EDWARD J. PHIPPS – *Stansfield*

On the nave wall of Stansfield Church, to the south of Bury St Edmunds, hangs a faded photograph of a Victorian incumbent with a bushy white beard and wearing a biretta – a little-known priest who was in his day a shining light of the Catholic revival and who knew and frequently corresponded with its leaders, J. H. Newman and E. B. Pusey. This was Edward James Phipps, Rector of Devizes, Wiltshire (1833-53) and of Stansfield, Suffolk (1854-84).

In 1840 he was summoned to appear before the Bishop of Salisbury for 'ritualistic practices' in his churches. His crimes were that he intoned the services, introduced the singing of the psalms and preached vested in a surplice.

He worked hard at Stansfield; although little that he did would today be called extreme, it was very new to Stansfield folk. He sang Matins daily at 7.00 or 8.00 am, for which he rang the church's three bells and presided at the organ, the congregation usually comprising his own family. By the 1870s he had established a weekly Eucharist following the third Collect at Morning Prayer, to which he insisted that his congregation should stay. Although a firm believer in vestments, fasting Communion and Confession, he did not try to impose these practices at Stansfield, but he used two lighted candles upon the altar and incense was burned before and during the services, although it was never used ceremonially.

He spearheaded the removal of the high box pews and the restoration of the church (by J. P. St Aubyn) in 1886. He held night schools and Sunday schools in the cart-shed at the Rectory. His son wrote that he faced bitter opposition throughout his time at Stansfield – the farmer at the Hall, who had definite Protestant sympathies, insisted upon sitting rigidly with his back to the altar at every service he attended. A stained glass window in memory of Fr Phipps shows a portrait of him as St Peter looking up at Christ. He had been crippled with rheumatism during the last five years of his ministry and he finally died following two paralytic strokes.

A later Rector here was the Rev'd Archie F. Webling, (1912-26) who came to this – his first parish – from a curacy at St Matthew, Southsea, with great ideas of turning it into a centre of the advanced Catholicism to which he was used. In the end he did not attempt to do so, but he gave the people Catholic teaching, as he continued to do at his future parish of Risby. Webling was a scholar, theologian and historian and his autobiography *Something Beyond* sincerely and sensitively describes how he dealt with the 'crises of faith' and the 'dark nights of the soul' – things that were very real to him and to many Christians.

CLEMENT W. D. CHEVALLIER – *Aspall*

Another priest who came to Suffolk as Vicar of a quiet village, having been trained in a busy town at a well-known advanced church, was Fr Clement Woodward Dumaresque Chevallier, who was Vicar of Aspall from 1902 to 1906. His family were lords of the Manor; Canon C. A. Chevallier, a leading Evangelical, was Vicar here from 1849-85. Fr Clement was Curate at St Olave, York and then, from 1898 to 1902, worked under the saintly Fr John Burn at All Saints, Middlesbrough where he took full part in the very advanced practices in that bastion of Catholicism in the North East. This extended to using the Roman custom of candidates taking on an extra Christian name at their Confirmation. Chevallier was known to have often insisted that all the boys whom he prepared for Confirmation should take his own name of Clement (thankfully not Dumaresque!), so that the confirming Bishop was presented with a long list of names – John Clement Brown, George Charles Clement Jones, etc. He was also a very talented violinist, who wrote an operetta, and he personally conducted a performance of this at Scarborough.

When he arrived at Aspall he attempted to form a Brotherhood of Youths from All Saints, much to the disgust of his brother who lived at the Hall and of his mother, who lived at the Old Rectory with him, and who objected to the young Yorkshire 'monks' bringing mud into the house! This was remedied by the lads scaling a ladder set against an upper window – in full view of the village street! An old postcard of Aspall Church's interior reveals that Fr Chevallier kept its furnishings very simple, but placed a large and prominent crucifix over the pulpit.

ROBERT H. FAULCONER – *Swilland and Trimley St Mary*

A little-known but very talented priest who left his mark upon two Suffolk churches was Robert Hoffman Faulconer. He had inherited a solicitor's practice but chose to take Holy Orders instead, serving a curacy at the Church of St Mary Magdalene, Lincoln before coming to the tiny church at Swilland in 1892. Here he set about completing the work of restoring and beautifying the church that Fr Bicknell (who had died ten years before) had begun. He had the porch rebuilt and added the distinctive top stage and spire to the tower, which was inspired by work that he had seen on the Continent. Many improvements were made to the interior, including stained glass windows in memory of four 19th-century rectors who preceded him, in which St Felix and St Richard both have the face of Bishop Edward King who had ordained him.

In 1897 he went to Trimley St Mary where he transformed what was then a very plain and rather sad-looking little church into a place of dignity, colour and atmosphere. When appealing for money to do this he wrote, 'this church, put into the hands of Mr Bodley or some other equally eminent architect, with £2,000 or £3,000 to restore, and Mr C. Kempe or Messrs Powell & Sons to glaze with their exquisite stained glass, could be made one of the most beautiful and interesting in East Anglia'. It was probably John Shewell Corder who supervised the work at Trimley and at Swilland but Mr Bodley would probably have approved because the workmanship and design are beautiful.

During his years at Trimley he did not take the worship into the extreme realms of ritualism, but the fact that he instituted a weekly early Communion service with a monthly second celebration, and celebrations on Thursdays, Saints days and other festivals (including Corpus Christi), clearly indicates the sacramental teaching which he gave there. The lavish sanctuary and reredos (and again Bishop King in stained glass) may well indicate that had he stayed longer, the worship might have advanced considerably.

He and Fr Cobbold were chosen to share in conducting the funeral of Fr Drury of Claydon in 1895. His own untimely death occurred in January 1904 'after many months of painful suffering cheerfully accepted'. Somebody wrote in his Service Register after his death, 'for a memorial, look around you, for he restored this church'. He had, in fact, been in poor health for several years, but in spite of this he was remembered as a very talented preacher with a lovable disposition, known especially for his friendly jokes and for the special love which he had for his poorer parishioners. He influenced Canon Pretyman to build a Parish Room at Trimley for the people. He was very keen on music and the organ case at Swilland shows his influence. He was also skilled with the needle and the elaborate needlework still to be seen at Swilland and Trimley was executed by him and his sister. During his last days he left careful instructions for his funeral, which took place at the 8.00 am Eucharist on a Sunday morning.

GEORGE A. COBBOLD – *St Bartholomew, Ipswich*

The foundation of St Bartholomew's was in some ways a family affair. Anna Frances Spooner, the second wife of the Rector of Hadleigh, was its founder and benefactress. She had learned the Catholic Faith at St Mary le Tower from Canon Turnock. Her husband's nephew, Charles Spooner, designed the great church, and her own nephew, George Augustus Cobbold, was its first Vicar. He was appointed in 1894, having served a curacy at Barnes. Although in public some thought him a rather shy and retiring man, this was far from true in terms of his attractive preaching, his versatile pen, and the quiet dynamism with which he firmly planted the Catholic Faith in the suburbia of eastern Ipswich. From 1899 until his death in 1915 he worked in partnership with his Curate, Fr Charles E. Curtis, and together they formed an effective team. Fr Curtis came here from St Saviour, Poplar, where he had been trained by no less a priest than Fr R. R. Dolling, so it is not surprising that he had a burning love of souls and was a tireless visitor who specialised in work with young men and boys.

Fr Cobbold was a scholar and the author of several books, but his parish magazines are probably his most appealing literary masterpieces. They are full of Catholic teaching put in a simple and challenging manner and are laced with wit and humour – something rarely seen in parochial journals at that time. From them we can trace how Fr Cobbold moulded the tradition at St Bartholomew's. Services at the beginning were Holy Communion at 8.00 am, Matins at

11.00 am and Evensong at 7.00 pm, with a second Celebration monthly following a 10.30 am Matins. There were celebrations also on Holy days. From this simple beginning, he gently but deliberately introduced changes when he felt that the people were ready for them.

He began to teach people in 1895 about fasting during Lent and explained the significance of the linen vestments and servers' robes that he was going to bring into use. The Confraternity of the Blessed Sacrament made a grant towards vestments for Communion on festivals and a branch of this society was formed at St Bartholomew's. He said that it was on the recommendation of the Archbishop of Canterbury that he used the Sarum colours and ceremonial in the new church, although he wore a biretta and there were six candles above the High Altar as well as a set of the Stations of the Cross. He looked forward to the use of incense, but stated that his principle in this and everything was 'to make no change without explanation'. The new church, although incomplete, was consecrated in December 1895 and the first Solemn celebration took place on Easter Day 1896. Fr Cobbold was by no means an ardent Papalist and in November 1896 he preached a sermon entitled 'Rome – the cause of a divided Christendom', about the Pope's encyclical on Anglican Orders *Apostolicæ Curæ*. The Patronal Festival in 1897 was a grand affair, with a High celebration, involving the choir and a small orchestra. It was recorded that at this service there were more than fifty candles burning around the High Altar. Fr A. H. Stanton of St Alban, Holborn preached in the evening – Fr Cobbold remarked that he had 'sat under him' for 25 years. Fr Cobbold had many friends among the clergy at the head of the Catholic Movement in London and elsewhere. Fr Dolling (of Landport fame), Fr Hogg of St Alban, Holborn, and Fr Ram of St John the Baptist, Timberhill, Norwich, were amongst several prominent people who occupied St Bartholomew's pulpit. He sold Christmas cards on behalf of the work done at St Peter, London Docks; its famous Vicar, Fr Lincoln Wainwright, not only preached at St Bartholomew's on two Sundays in 1913 but also conducted Fr Cobbold's funeral two years later. The leading Catholic Layman, Mr Athelston Riley, wrote the preface to his book *Why I am an Anglo-Catholic,* which Mowbrays published in 1908.

By 1899 there was a weekly Sung Mass, and by 1901, a daily Mass. Other services gradually took their places in St Bartholomew's curriculum of events, including Tenebræ on Good Friday, Midnight Mass at Christmas and the Blessing and Distribution of Palms, which (the Vicar remarked) was the service that always produced the largest congregation of the year. He usually took his annual holiday on the Continent where he enjoyed visiting churches and cathedrals. Italy was a favourite venue and on one trip to Rome he examined 100 churches.

He endured much opposition, although nothing like the riots at Claydon, and he held rather narrow views about Protestantism. He opposed the Fair held in Ipswich on Good Friday which he saw as sacrilege and he believed that 'Protestantism of the worst sort is at the bottom of it'; but he seemed to regard the Kensitites, who were constantly badgering him and the Faith for which he stood, as a challenge. They gave scope for outbursts of his impish wit in his magazine. Yet he was not averse to poking honest fun at himself. In his Vicar's Letter he once wrote 'Sometimes I am afraid my letter is dull enough to bear keeping a fortnight before it sees the light' and, following a newspaper report of a service at St Bartholomew's, 'services at St Bartholomew's would never have struck me as "weird", nor was I aware that I was "retiring" – tiring I think I would have understood'.

CLAUDE T. G. POWELL – *St Bartholomew, Ipswich*

Claude Tringham Graham Powell was a Suffolk lad who had lived at Southwold from the age of three and he succeeded Fr Cobbold in 1916. He started his ministry at St John the Divine, Kennington and, after a further curacy at Odd Rode, Cheshire, was parish priest of Shipmeadow for twelve years before coming to St Bartholomew's. Under him this church became one of the sentinels of the Catholic Movement in East Anglia. Missions were held, a variety of guilds set up, and from the outset of his ministry the Western Use replaced the Sarum Use at St Bartholomew. Fr Cobbold's abiding wish that the Blessed Sacrament should be reserved in the church was fulfilled shortly after his successor had arrived. At Patronal festivals there was usually a great procession along Felixstowe Road. Parish pilgrimages to Walsingham took place and the church interior was greatly beautified. Although Fr Powell was seen to represent Catholicism, triumphant and unashamed, the esteem in which his fellow clergy held him is seen in his election as a Proctor in Convocation and to the Church Assembly, and in his Honorary Canonry of his Cathedral. He was also one of the few married Guardians of the Shrine of Our Lady of Walsingham, having been an enthusiastic supporter of the Shrine since pilgrimages were revived in the 1920s. He can be seen in the photographs of the great procession in 1931 when the statue was carried from Walsingham parish church to the new Pilgrimage Church.

ROBERT A. J. SUCKLING – *Barsham*

Several rectors of this small north Suffolk village were members of the Suckling family, who had been lords of the Manor and Patrons of the Living there since 1623. Robert Alfred John Suckling's father had been the first Incumbent of Bussage, Gloucestershire, whose church was erected in 1846 by some of the leaders of the Oxford Movement at the suggestion of J. H. Newman. Robert was Rector of Barsham from 1868 to 1880. His Godfather was John Keble, who wrote to Edward King, Robert's Principal at Cuddesdon, 'it is delightful to hear such good accounts of Suckling. The son of so many prayers ought to do well'. In 1880 he left Barsham to accept the challenge of a vastly different parish and went to St Peter, London Docks. Two years later he began his 34-year ministry at St Alban, Holborn. Whilst there, in addition to his very memorable ministry in this stronghold of the Catholic Faith, he succeeded Dr Pusey as Warden of Ascot Priory and was for a time Master of the Society of the Holy Cross.

We know little of his ministry at Barsham; there were no riots or sensations, but one item from Barsham, now in the County Archives, is of interest. It is a small velvet wallet, which contains a testimonial that speaks a great deal of Fr Suckling. It accompanied a pair of candlesticks which his parishioners presented to him for the High Altar in Barsham Church in 1872, 'in gratitude to Almighty God for the many spiritual blessings that we have received in the

Blessed Sacrament of the Altar and as a token of our affection for you, who have taught us by word and example to value these blessings … We hope that you will consider it consistent with your duty to use them with lighted candles in memory of His incarnate Nature whom we there adore as the Light of the World'.

Fr Suckling retained his love for his little Suffolk church and was generous to it, both during and after his ministry there. Much of what we now see in the church was given by him.

ALLAN COATES – *Barsham*

Fr Allan Coates came to Barsham in 1889. He was a scholarly priest with a love of ancient and beautiful things. He caused the north aisle to be rebuilt, he designed the High Altar reredos and acquired furnishings and adornments of the highest quality to make the interior atmospheric and beautiful. Some items came from other English churches and some from the continent. The generosity of Fr Suckling was a great help to him in his transformation of the church.

He came to Barsham from a curacy at St Barnabas, Oxford and his love of beauty and antiquity showed itself not only in the church building but also in the services here. The procession, which preceded the *Missa Cantata* on the feast of the Holy Name, was described for the Commission for Clergy Discipline in 1904. It was a beautifully rendered act, with crucifer, thurifer, acolytes and servers all in albs and amices. He also instituted a Procession of Palms and a Rogation Procession around the churchyard. The Liturgy and Reproaches took place on Good Friday and there was Vespers of the Blessed Sacrament at Corpus Christi. In the County Archives are preserved his detailed and scholarly history of the church, and the little book in which he recorded his services between 1903 and 1911 which is headed '✠ *Acta Ecclesiæ Sacrosanctæ Trinitatis de Barsham*'. An entry in November 1905 records 'Rector to Beccles Hospital for amputation of leg', and three months later, whilst he was still out of action, the church was struck by lightning and the altar wrecked.

Barsham – Sanctuary following the lightning strike in 1906.

Under his guidance, however, and G. F. Bodley's superintendence, all the damage was successfully repaired. He was soon mobile again, equipped with a wooden leg and driving his familiar pony and trap around the parish.

Amongst the gifts and furnishings placed in Barsham Church during his time were:

• A sanctuary lamp, given by Fr Williams of Ufford
• The font cover from Ellingham Church
• A cope, white frontal, wall hangings and dossal, six candlesticks and two chandeliers from Antwerp, all given by the Rector
• A Litany Desk made up from mediæval woodwork from Mettingham and Heckingham churches
• A 16th-century Processional Cross, 18th-century French standard candlesticks and pewter candlesticks from Strasbourg
• A lectern which was formerly in the library of Merton College, Oxford
• Altar rails for the side chapel from Southwold Church, the hinge to their gate having come from a Rhineland church and given by F. C. Eden.

HERBERT DRAKE – *Braiseworth and Ufford*

In 1897, Fr Aelred Carlyle – who was later to found the Anglican Benedictine Community on the Island of Caldey – had a small community-in-the-making, which was then resident at Guiting Power in Gloucestershire where it had started a Rescue Home for boys. Fr Aelred invited Herbert Drake to be the resident Chaplain and Spiritual Director and, as "Fr Anselm OSB" he served St Bernard's Monastery at Guiting for five months, until Protestant agitators caused such havoc that the scheme had to be abandoned and Fr Anselm returned to secular ministry. Both at Guiting and in his earlier position (attached to the East Grinstead Sisters' Home for the Dying at Clapham Common) he was used to such extreme customs as giving Benediction with a monstrance.

After a few short curacies he came to Braiseworth in 1907 as its parish priest and here he raised the churchmanship considerably. He also founded St Christopher's Home for Boys, which was opened and blessed in 1914, but had closed before 1922. He left in 1919 to begin his long and effective ministry at Ufford. He is also remembered as a keen and expert campanologist.

LEIGHTON SANDYS WASON – Assistant Curate – *Elmswell*

One of England's most remarkable and most eccentric priests, whose story is tinged with sadness. Fr Leighton Sandys Wason was single-minded and outspoken and for most of his long life he had to endure the extreme disfavour of the Anglican Establishment, whilst courageously upholding his deep and sincere convictions.

He came to Elmswell for a three-year period (1894-7) as Fr Hipwell's Curate. Throughout this time, however, he remained in Deacon's orders because Bishop Compton of Ely refused to ordain him Priest until he gave up the use of the Rosary. He moved to St Andrew, Plaistow where he was Priested and then to the very extreme church of St Michael, Shoreditch. His only living was Cury and Gunwalloe, Cornwall, where he stayed from 1905 until he was deprived of it in 1919. Although he was never offered another parish, and it was not until 1943 that any bishop would even license him to officiate, he still clung to the Catholic Faith for which he had fought and suffered and many of his friends all over the country were only too pleased to welcome him to their churches, including Fr Drake of Ufford. An uncompromising papalist, Fr Wason vehemently campaigned for the service of Benediction which several Anglican churches now enjoy without persecution. He also distinguished himself as a writer of novels and as a poet. His old friend, Fr Bernard Walke of St Hilary, Cornwall, recorded some of his lovable eccentricities, including the period in his life when he acquired an old firm of church publishers called Cope & Fenwick and rented premises in central London where he sold books and "pieties". He came to Needham Market to assist Fr Hargrave Thomas during World War Two and in 1943 Bishop Brook restored his licence to officiate. He lived to celebrate the Golden Jubilee of his Priesthood and died in 1950, aged 83 years.

FREDERICK E. WARREN, MA, BD, FSA, Hon DD – *Bardwell*

Dr Warren was a graduate and Fellow of St John's College, Oxford and one of the great academics amongst the Suffolk Anglo-Catholic clergy of his time. His teaching and practice whilst Rector of Bardwell (1890-1922) appear to have been in the old Tractarian tradition and were certainly not advanced, although he was for many years the Chairman of the Bury Branch of the English Church Union. He had been Vice Principal of Chichester Theological College 1871-3 and came to Bardwell from the parish of Frenchay, Gloucestershire. He was the author of several scholarly works on ancient rites and liturgies, including such intriguing titles as *The Old Catholic Ritual, done into English and compared with the corresponding Liturgies in the Roman and Old German Manuals, The Liturgy and Ritual of the Old Catholic Church* and *The Sarum Missal in English*. He retired from Bardwell to East Molesey, Surrey.

WILLIAM G. HARGRAVE THOMAS – *Needham Market*

There is no churchyard to this noble, barn-like 15th-century church, because until 1901 it was a Chapel of Ease for Barking Church. Beneath one of the grandest and most unusual mediæval roofs in England were, until many were swept away after 1964, a host of ornaments and aids to devotion, including Stations of the Cross, statues, pictures and two beautifully adorned side altars facing north and south against the nave walls. A handsome oak rood-loft and rood figures were erected in 1953 but the intended screen beneath them was never built.

The Rev'd W. G. Hargrave Thomas (1925-64) was one of Suffolk's unforgettable characters. I met him several times in the period just before he retired, aged 76, after nearly 40 years at Needham. Thin, wiry, but with bright eyes, and armed with peppermints of unknown vintage to share with any young people whom he encountered, he found in me an eager listener to his ecclesiastical anecdotes. He once told me how to discern the churchmanship of a priest by the thickness of his collar, pointing out to me that his own was a tiny strip, only half an inch thick!

The radical ideas of this gifted and energetic priest were either liked or loathed, but few people disliked the man himself or failed to be impressed by his personality, his humour, his many skills or his deep spirituality. A native of Birmingham and trained at Lampeter and Cuddesdon, he served curacies at St Michael, Handsworth and St Alban, Bordesley (Birmingham), then became a Missionary Priest in the diocese of Zanzibar, before coming to Needham Market. One wonders what this little town in 1925 made of their new Vicar, who was a passionate Socialist and a convinced Anglo-Catholic. He was active in local government and became a parish Councillor, and was elected to Gipping Rural District Council and East Suffolk County Council, becoming an Alderman in 1946. The year after he arrived he crossed his bishop when he addressed some 2,000 participants in the General Strike on Ipswich Cornhill. He lived and preached the Social Gospel, as so many of the great slum-priests did, believing that the confessional and other aspects of his ministry taught him about real people and their needs. It is said that a stranger knocking at his door would be asked, "What do you want – money, food or clothing?" – and always they received what they asked for.

He had discovered the Catholic Faith as a lad when he visited a church in Small Heath, Birmingham and he never looked back. He wrote, 'When I attended the High Mass I knew that I had at last come home!' And this he practised in all its fullness at Needham Market for 40 years – a ministry enriched by his talents as a musician, historian and preacher. His retirement in 1964 marked the end of an era there. His *Recollections of a Suffolk Vicar* makes interesting reading. In 1942 he welcomed the exiled and "inhibited" Fr Sandys Wason as his Assistant Priest and managed to persuade Bishop Brook to grant him a licence to minister legally after 23 years in exile.

Frs Wason, right, and Walke (parish priest of St Hilary, Cornwall), about to play tennis.

Fr Wason in later life.

Suffolk Clergy who appeared in the *Ritualistic Clergy List,* 1903

THE PROTESTANT WING produced this Directory of Clergy in order to expose those clergy who adopted any of the *Six Points of Ritual* (with the exception of wafer bread), or who belonged to any of the four *Romanising Societies,* all of which are abbreviated beside their names thus:

ECU   = Member of the English Church Union
ex ECU   = Member in 1901 but subsequently not so.
CBS   = Priest Associate of the Confraternity of the Blessed Sacrament
SSJE   = Member of the Society of St John the Evangelist *(Cowley Fathers)*
SSC   = Member of the Society of the Holy Cross *(Societas Sanctæ Crucis)*

E   = Adopts the Eastward Position
M   = Uses the Mixed Chalice
I   = Uses incense
V   = Wears Eucharistic vestments
L   = Uses lighted candles for services in daylight.

NAME	PARISH	SOCIETIES	RITUAL
Allan, G.	Kenton	*ex* ECU	E, M, V, L
Archer, G. F.	Whitton		E, M, L
Badeley, G. E.	Great Whelnetham		E, M
Barber, R. W.	Thurston	ECU, SSC, CBS	E, M
Barker, R. V.	Bramford & Burstall		E, M, L
Barnes, W. E. M.	*Curate,* All Ss Newmarket	ECU	E
Barrington, Y. A.	St Mary le Tower, Ipswich		E, M, V, L
Bartrum, H. H.	Alpheton	ECU	E, M, L
Betham, C. J.	Brettenham		E, M, L
Bignold, R. A.	Carlton Colville		E, M, L
Birch, H. W.	Ipswich (retired)	ECU, CBS	
Blakiston, R. M.	Hadleigh		E, M, L
Bourne, H. C.	St Mary, Newmarket		E, L
Boycott, G. A. B.	*Curate,* Carlton Colville	ECU	M, E, L
Braybrook, W. A. R.	*Curate,* Lavenham	*ex* ECU	E
Brown, J. W. D.	Stowlangtoft		E

NAME	PARISH	SOCIETIES	RITUAL
Cahusac, F. H.	Thorpe Morieux	ECU	E, M
Campbell, C. A. F.	Thornham		E, M
Cartwright, A. B.	Icklingham		E, M, V, L
Champion, G. J.	*Curate*, Kirkley	ECU, CBS	
Chevallier, C. W. D.	Aspall	ECU, CBS	E, M, I, V, L
Clarkson, C. B.	Lawshall		E
Coates, A.	Barsham	ECU, CBS	E, M, I, V, L
Cobbold, G. A.	St Bartholomew, Ipswich	ECU, CBS	E, M, I, V, L
Cockayne, H.	Kirkley	ECU, CBS	E, M, V, L
Coller, R. M.	Hasketon	ECU	E, M, V, L
Colville, W. W.	St Agnes, Newmarket		E, M, V, L
Cooper, J.	Corton	CBS	E
Copeland, R. M.	*Curate*, Ufford	ECU, CBS	E, M, I, V, L
Coyle, R. J.	*Curate*, St Mary le Tower, Ipswich		E, M, V, L
Crean, A.	*Curate*, St Gregory & St Peter, Sudbury		E, L
Curtis, C. E.	*Curate*, St Barts, Ipswich	ECU, CBS	E, M, I, V, L
Dale, G.	All Ss, Newmarket	CBS	E
Davies, G. H. D.	Kelsale	*ex* ECU	E, V, L
Davies, J.	Charsfield		E, V, L
Davies, R. D.	Kettleburgh		E, M, I, V, L
Deane, H. J.	*Curate*, Leiston		E, M, V, L
Denman-Dean, R.	St Mary, Woodbridge		E, L
Dennett, F. S.	*Curate*, St John, Bury St Edmunds		E, L
Dennis, G. T.	Hopton (nr Diss)	ECU	E, M, L
Dickenson, L. G. T.	Brome		E, M, V, L
Downton, C.	Hoxne		E, M, L
Downton, F. M.	*Curate*, St Mary, Stoke, Ipswich		E, M, L
Doxat, F.	Woolverstone	ECU, CBS	
Durrant, C. R.	Freston		E, M
Elliott, C. L. B.	Tattingstone		E, L
Faulconer, R. H.	Trimley St Mary	*ex* ECU, CBS	
Fletcher, W. E.	St Matthew, Ipswich		E
Fryer, R. S.	Rougham		E, L

NAME	PARISH	SOCIETIES	RITUAL
Gathercole, M. A.	Santon Downham	ECU	E, M, L
Gillmor, A. H.	*Curate,* St Gregory, Sudbury	ECU	
Gipps, H. F.	Hundon	ECU	E, M, V, L
Grant, A. R.	Hitcham		E, M, L
Gray, A. W.	St Andrew, Rushmere		E, L
Gray, J. D.	Nayland	ECU, CBS	E, M, V, L
Gray, W. B.	Kersey		E, I, L
Griffith, E. H.	Wickham Market	ECU, CBS	E, M, V, L
Hair, A. C.	*Curate,* Long Melford		E, M, V, L
Hall, H.	Glemsford		E
Hall, H. J.	*Curate,* Haverhill		E, M, V, L
Harris, W. H.	Mendham	ECU, CBS	E, M, L
Havard, L. L.	Alpheton *(retired)*	*ex* ECU	
Hawkins, E. W.	Ringshall	ECU	E
Hedges, P.	St Matthew, Kirkley	ECU, CBS	E, M, L
Hill, H. C.	Buxhall		E, M, V, L
Hipwell, J.	Elmswell	ECU, CBS, SSC	E, M, V, L
Hodges, G.	St James, Bury St Edmunds		E, M, L
Hooper, W.	Great & Little Glemham	ECU	E, M, L
Horne, F. H.	Drinkstone	ECU	
Horsfall, F. H.	*Curate,* Hitcham	*ex* ECU	E, M, L
Housecroft, T.	Great Finborough		E, L
Jervis, W. H. E. R.	Bures		E, M
Johnson, A. C.	Capel St Mary	CBS	E, M, I, V, L
Jones, A.	Claydon	ECU	E, M, V, L
Kemp, J.	Haughley	ECU	E, M, L
King, E. S.	*Curate,* Sudbury	ECU	E, L
Kirby, W. H.	Woolpit	ECU, CBS	E, M, V, L
Leeper, W. C.	Mellis	ECU	E, M, L
Lucas, H. J. A.	Melton		E
Milne, E. A.	Wyverstone	ECU	
Munday, J. G.	St John, Felixstowe		E, M, L
Murray, M. W.	*Curate,* Bramford		E, M, L

NAME	PARISH	SOCIETIES	RITUAL
Nash, C. B.	Yaxley		E, M, V, L
Nettleship, W. B.	Brockley		E, M, V, L
Normandale, T.	*Curate,* Cavendish		E, L
Nunn, D. P. R.	Hessett	ECU, CBS	E, M, V, L
Oliver, W. R. J. H.	St Margaret, Ilketshall		E
Olorenshaw, J. R.	Rattlesden		E, M, L
Osborne, E. A.	*Curate,* Worlingworth	*ex* ECU, CBS	
Packard, O. B.	Depden	ECU	
Parker, Sir W. H.	Long Melford Hall	ECU	
Pearson, A. C.	Ringsfield		E, M, L
Phillips, F. A.	Gorleston	CBS	E, I, V, L
Pilter, W. T.	Gedding		E
Powell, F.	*Curate,* St John, Felixstowe		E, M, L
Pywell, W. A.	Wixoe	ECU	
Raper, N. J.	*Curate,* St Mary, Stoke, Ipswich		E, M, L
Raven, B. W.	Leiston		E, M, V, L
Robbs, A.	*Curate,* Woodbridge		E, L
Rutter, J. H.	Haverhill		E, M, V
Sawbridge, J. S.	Thelnetham	ECU	E, M, L
Scott, E. M.	Sudbourne & Orford	ECU	E, M, L
Scott, H. M.	*Curate,* Coddenham & Crowfield		E, M, L
Scott, T.	Lavenham		E
Sellon, W. S.	Kettlebaston	ECU, CBS, SSC	E, M, I, V, L
Sharland, G. F.	*Curate,* Buxhall	*ex* ECU	
Sherlock, H. E.	Bildeston		E, M, L
Singleton, W. F.	Great Cornard		E, M, V, L
Smith, W. M.	St Cross, South Elmham		E
Spencer, A. J.	Eye		E, L
Stantial, A. E.	Bacton		E, L
Stantial, T.	St John, Bury St Edmunds	ECU	E, L
Steele, C.	Leavenheath		E, M
Stephenson, E. H. C.	Assington		E
Stretton, J. G. M.	*Curate-in-Charge,* West Row		E
Sutherland, A. H.	*Curate,* St John, Bury St Edmunds		E, L

NAME	PARISH	SOCIETIES	RITUAL
Taylor, H.	*Curate,* St James, Bury St Edmunds		E, M, L
Thomas, L. J.	Swilland	ECU	E, M, I, V, L
Titcombe, J. C.	*Chaplain,* Seckford Hospital		
	Woodbridge	*ex* ECU, CBS, SSJE	
Tompson, R.	St Mary, Stoke, Ipswich	ECU	E, M, L
Townson, R.	*Ex-Rector,* Gedding	*ex* ECU, CBS	
Tuck, J. G.	Tostock	ECU, CBS	E, M, L
Vatcher, J. R. M.	Clare		E, M, L
Vawdrey, J. C.	Kessingland		E, M
Walker, H. A.	Chattisham	ECU, CBS	
Wall, C. de R.	*Curate,* St Matthew, Ipswich	*ex* ECU	E
Warren, F. E.	Bardwell	ECU, CBS	E, M, V, L
Watson, A. H.	Nacton & Levington	ECU	E, M
West, A. P. F.	Edwardstone		E, L
White, A. K.	Great Saxham	*ex* ECU	E, M
Wild, E. J.	Rattlesden		E, M, L
Wilkinson, A. A.	Hintlesham		E, M, L
Wilkinson, H. B.	Chelsworth	ECU, CBS, SSC	E, M, V, L
Wilkinson, H. R.	Stoke by Nayland		E, M
Williams, H.	Ufford	ECU, CBS, SSC	E, M, I, V, L
Wilson, J. R.	Cavendish		E, L
Wilson, W. L.	Rumburgh		E
Wodehouse, A.	Chelmondiston		E, M, V, L
Wood, A. S. H.	Beyton	ECU	
Wood, F.	Erwarton		E, M, V, L
Wood, W. H.	Mildenhall		E, L
Wood, W. J.	St Andrew, Ilketshall	ECU	E, M, L
Woolley, H. B.	*Curate,* Mildenhall	ECU, CBS	E, L
Woolsey, J. J.	Brightwell & Kesgrave	ECU	E, M, L
Wyles, W.	Coddenham & Crowfield		E, M, L
Yonge, C. F. L.	Shottisham	ECU, CBS	E, V, L
Young, J. H.	Shipmeadow	ECU, CBS	E, M, V, L

Chapter Five

Religious Communities in Suffolk

ONE OF THE FRUITS of the Catholic Revival was the revival of the monastic life in the Anglican Church. Now many communities of monks and nuns offer up prayer and intercession and also do much skilful and necessary work for the Church and for the world. Countless people have cause to be thankful to these dedicated people who have taken the three-fold vow of Poverty, Chastity and Obedience for their loving care in nursing, teaching, tending the poor and outcasts, lavishing skill upon making vestments and church requisites, conducting retreats and missions, writing books, offering hospitality, or simply for the constant rendering of praise and prayer. Despite all this, the early attempts to revive the monastic life were fraught with opposition and some schemes failed miserably.

In Suffolk, monasticism in a rather eccentric, anachronistic and individualistic form was to make its appearance through the pioneering work of Joseph Leycester Lyne, alias Father Ignatius OSB, who began his one-man attempt to re-establish the Benedictine order in the Anglican Church at Claydon Rectory. He was surrounded by aggravation wherever he went and was hindered by lack of recognition or encouragement by the Anglican Establishment, violent opposition by protestants and his own gullibility which failed to detect potential evil in some of the characters who joined his monastery. Conversely he was rather pig-headed and was convinced that every decision that he made was the direct guidance of the Holy Spirit, so he had no sense of business, he rarely listened to advice and he totally ignored authority, whilst imposing it rigidly himself. He was nevertheless a remarkable man – a gifted "Revivalist" preacher, a talented musician and a prolific writer. For most of his ministry he was a freelance Deacon, until late in his life, when he received valid, but irregular, Priest's orders at the hands of the exotic Mar Timotheus – an *Episcopus Vagans* (literally a wandering bishop), and this destroyed much of the credibility he once had.

On Shrove Tuesday 1863, Ignatius and two young men arrived at Claydon, ready to begin Benedictine monasticism with all its undiluted mediæval rigours. The monks soon increased to six, and were woken up at 2.00 am by their Superior for the first of the many monastic offices that punctuated their day.

These were taken from a manuscript copy (dating from the 17th century) of the *Breviarium Monasticum,* which was translated from the Latin, impromptu on the spot. The psalms were from the *Book of Common Prayer* and the hymns from Helmore's *Hymnal Noted.* Poor Fr Drury, whilst he was delighted with the advanced ceremonial, the thought of real monks in his parish, their help in the school and Ignatius' help with parochial duties, had nevertheless taken on a great deal. Ignatius was above worrying about mundane things like money or avoiding causing inconvenience. The Drurys' cook had to provide special meals for the monks, which were eaten apart from the family, although the Brethren enjoyed playing with the Drury children and pushing the little ones around the garden in a four-wheeled chaise. On 30 January 1864, the Benedictine order made its departure to new premises at Elm Hill, Norwich, and 16 months of further publicity, persecution and problems. It was not until 1870 that the foundation stone was laid for their permanent monastery – the new Llanthony Abbey – in the Black Mountains.

Fr Drury did not give up his interest in monasticism and in 1866 he established a community of Benedictine nuns, who ran a school for children of all classes. Their Superior was Mary Ware, who bought a large house in the main street of Claydon and conveyed it to Fr Drury for use as a convent. This house stands on the east side of the old Norwich road – it later became the Rectory and is now in private hands. In 1882 Fr Drury and Miss Ware had 'differences'! Drury felt that the convent was not being run according to his original wishes and wanted it disbanded. Both parties agreed that the house should be transferred back to Miss Ware, on condition that it was not used as a convent or for religious services. Some of the nuns joined convents throughout the country.

The Rev'd John Mason Neale sent a few Sisters from his Convent of St Margaret at East Grinstead to work amongst the poor in the vast parish of St Matthew, Ipswich, where they set up their Sisterhood of St Mary the Virgin in 1857. Fr Neale paid a day visit to the Sisters and his 'genial, loving nature' fascinated the 100 or so children with whom they worked. In an afternoon session with them the great hymn-writer and translator was asked how hymns and songs were created. 'It is all very easy', he replied – and there and then composed an on-the-spot hymn especially for them:

I am a little Catholic,
And Christian is my name,
And I believe in Holy Church,
In every age the same.

And I believe the English Church,
To be a part of her,
The Holy Church throughout the world,
That cannot fail or err.

And ever since Augustine came,
The Gospel here to bring,
And spake beneath an ancient oak,
To Ethelbert the king;

And taught him of one God on high,
By all to be adored,
And of our Saviour, Jesus Christ,
His only Son, our Lord;

There have been churches on the hill,
And churches in the vale,
And churches on the high white cliff,
By which the good ships sail.

And here as well, in this our town,
Full many a church have we:
St Matthew and St Margaret,
And St Mary by the Quay.

God bless them all, and bless their Priests,
And grant us of His Love,
That all who help the Church on earth,
May join the Church above.

The Rector of St Matthew's, the Rev'd Charles Gaye, was described by contemporary newspapers as a 'Puseyite' and was clearly in sympathy with the early ideals of the Oxford Movement, although he did not do a great deal to advance the ritual in his church. He had the care of a very large parish, containing many small tenements inhabited by poor people, and clearly this was just the sort of environment in which a dedicated band of Sisters could do untold good; so when they willingly offered their services, Gaye, after careful thought, welcomed them.

It seems that during the year or so that they spent in the parish, the Sisters worked hard for the people, nursing the sick, teaching the young and carrying out innumerable acts of mercy. They lived their community life in premises in the parish. Unfortunately their presence annoyed several of Mr Gaye's parishioners and there exists a long letter which he wrote to one person saying that he knew he risked causing offence by sanctioning the Sisters' presence in the parish, but that he was sure that if only the parishioner would wait a while and see the work that they did, he would change his mind and become one of their most ardent supporters. Mr Gaye was clearly no lover of what he referred to as the 'erroneous Church of Rome', but urged his parishioners to 'have done with the childish fallacy that a thing is wrong, merely because it was adopted by the Church of Rome'.

The presence of the Sisters appeared to cause such opposition, however, that in 1858 Gaye had to ask them to leave. He gave as his reasons for doing so that he was popularly held to be directly responsible for them and he had not the time to devote to all the tasks which were involved in being their Director, and that the Lady Superior was not prepared to make any concessions about things which he considered to be non-essentials and which he saw as hindering his work in the parish. So, in mid-Lent in 1858, the Mother Superior wrote a letter to 'Our Friends and Neighbours, the Poor of the Parish of St Matthew, Ipswich' saying, 'Now the time has come when (at the wish of your Rector) we must lay aside our work and bid you farewell. We thank you again and again for the many tokens of affectionate gratitude we have received at your hands. We wish to forget all the hard words and unjust accusations that have been brought against us and to say our parting words to you with nothing but love in our hearts'.

In 1854, a Penitentiary (or House of Mercy) for "fallen" women was opened in a farmhouse (now Nunnery Farm) in the tiny village of Shipmeadow. The opening Eucharist took place in the parish church with thirty clergy present. The Chaplain to the House of Mercy was the Rector of Shipmeadow, the Rev'd Maurice Shelton Suckling. There was a comfortable little chapel in the house and pleasant accommodation for the young ladies in residence, who were kept very busy during the day. Their work included cord and twine making; they also received instruction and their meals were eaten in silence. The first Superior (a Miss Cozens, who had run a penitentiary at Clewer) was, after a short time, succeeded by Miss Lavinia Crosse, the daughter of a Norwich surgeon and a lady with strong determination. She was the driving force behind the staff of the penitentiary forming themselves into a sisterhood. This development did not meet with universal approval: the Governing Council said that they could not recognise a sisterhood and the Chaplain thought it polite to resign. Somebody informed one of the local newspapers of the proposal and several articles and letters of a very "anti" flavour ensued. On New Year's Eve 1855, however, Miss Crosse took her Life Vows before Canon T. T. Carter of Clewer, becoming the Mother Superior, and two ladies were professed as novices. This was the beginning of the Community of All Hallows.

Because the Shipmeadow house was not very suitable for health reasons, an appeal was launched for a new building and the new Chaplain, the Rev'd William Scudamore, secured a site in his parish of Ditchingham, on the Norfolk side of the Waveney. The foundation stone was laid in November 1856 and the new buildings, designed by Henry Woodyer, were opened in 1859. So the Community moved across the Waveney where, after a history of marvellous work in a variety of fields, the Sisters still continue to serve the Church, both at Ditchingham and in the city of Norwich.

In 1889, the Community opened the Lodge of the Good Shepherd on the outskirts of Ipswich, and also, in 1892, St Saviour's Lodge, Foundation Street, Ipswich. These houses offered medical treatment, rescue and rehabilitation to "fallen" women. The Good Shepherd Hostel closed shortly after 1895 and St Saviour's lasted until 1909. Fr Wakefield of Woolverstone was one of the first Chaplains at St Saviour's.

At Woolverstone itself was St Peter's Home of Rest, built by Charles Berners, the Squire, in 1902, for Anglican Sisters of all communities or, when a vacancy occurred, for any lady Church Worker. This became a hospital during World War I and was later converted into a private house.

Kettlebaston provided a home for two small religious communities for short periods of time. When the Benedictine nuns of St Bride's Abbey, Milford Haven, seceded to the Roman Catholic Church in 1913, a few who remained loyal to the Church of England set up the tiny Community of St Mary and St Scholastica. Having occupied several houses in Kent, they finally retired, in about 1920, to Kettlebaston.

The Sisterhood of the Holy Childhood was founded in 1881, mainly to work amongst children in needy parishes. There were two Houses – the Mother House at Clapham and a smaller House at Kettlebaston. Here a small group of children lived and were cared for by the Sisters. The community finished its work about 1930.

The Community of St Michael and All Angels was founded in 1895 in the parish of St Peter, Hammersmith, to offer a teaching ministry in schools. About 1907 they opened an independent House and Boarding School in what was the old Grammar School, Northgate Street, Bury St Edmunds. This became known as St Michael's College and the Sisters also helped in St John's parish. After the death of the Reverend Mother Ethel Mary in 1945 the school closed. It was she who had made most of the early vestments in use at St John's Church.

A considerable contribution to the Catholic Movement's role in missionary work, also in its pioneer work with theological colleges to train priests, has been made by the Society of the Sacred Mission, founded by Fr Herbert Kelly. This was organised and run as a religious community and began life as the Korean Missionary Brotherhood in 1890 at a house in the parish of St John the Divine at Kennington. The Founder was professed as a monk in 1894, by which time the Brotherhood had become the Society of the Sacred Mission. In 1897, at the suggestion of Canon Bullock Webster (Chaplain to the Bishop of Ely), the Society – which by then had about 13 students – moved to the 16th-century Manor House at Mildenhall, with the blessing of the Bishop of Ely and the Incumbent of Mildenhall. There it developed and grew, offering training for lay work and also to fit men for ordination. By 1901 there were 40 people accommodated at Mildenhall and larger premises were needed. In 1903, therefore, the Society moved to Kelham, near Newark, where it has done wonderful work for the Church. Kelham's unfortunate closure during recent years means that the Society's main house is now in Durham; some of the books from its library have found a home in the Library at Norwich Cathedral.

Chapter Six

Opposition and Persecution

THE STORY of the Catholic Revival is laced with tales of almost unbelievable persecution and intolerance. Anglo-Catholics were regarded with tremendous suspicion and their eventual influence upon the Anglican Church has been the result of great perseverance despite opposition by people who resented change, or who feared that it was all a sell-out to Rome, which was of course the ultimate evil in the eyes of sound Protestants, of which there were very many in Suffolk. These people were genuinely furious, and the externals in particular, such as vestments, incense and candles fanned their fury and they were determined to stamp out this Romeward Movement – hence the cries heard in Suffolk, 'We don't want no Popery here!'

In some cases their protests went far beyond letters to newspapers or official complaints to the Bishop. Services of worship were disturbed, churches were attacked and physical violence was threatened (and occasionally delivered) to clergy and people. On paper many of the Catholic innovations could have been considered illegal and the protests caused a great deal of worry to the bishops who were often forced into action in order to keep the peace. Leading Anglican Evangelicals, in 1865, formed the Church Association to maintain Protestant ideals and to put down Ritualism. The Protestant Truth Society, founded by John Kensit and still in operation today, has also done its utmost to expose ritualistic practices.

Suffolk's most vehement Protestant agitation was centred upon Claydon, particularly during 1863 and 1864, when Fr Ignatius was in residence there and made the parish infamous for its advanced practices. The ringing of the church bell day and night to call the monks to their offices and to sound out the *Angelus,* the remarkable outdoor processions with banners and incense, the cowled monks, the "goings-on" in the church, all put together constituted something which was almost unknown in an English village. What was more, people were also subjected to the Superior's riveting but hard-hitting preaching; his warnings of hell-fire and damnation, which matched any revivalist preacher, but which gave grave offence to many Suffolk folk who were not prepared to be told things like this by a monk, and who called Ignatius "Father Blazer". Ignatius, of course, considered himself responsible to God alone and felt that he had absolutely no need to seek Bishop Pelham's permission either to preach in Claydon church or to begin the national revival of the Anglican Benedictines in his diocese! Upon hearing of the disturbances at Claydon, the Bishop wrote to Fr Drury forbidding him to allow Ignatius to preach in his church.

The disturbances were frightful. People came from far and near to hear "Ignatius of Jesus" and Claydon became a focus of pilgrimage for crowds. Some came out of pious motives, others out of curiosity to catch a glimpse of the "monkery" in the Suffolk village; there were also loyal Protestants who came fired with a desire to abolish the "mummeries of superstition". The local farming community, mostly of Protestant stock, encouraged their employees and tenants to make life hell for the monks. One wealthy landowner offered £1,000 to anybody who could finally destroy 'this hornet's nest'. For the price of a pint, many sturdy Suffolk yokels were enlisted for "rent-a-crowd" to cause as much trouble as possible. Fr Drury had stones and other missiles hurled at him and so did the windows of his church. Ignatius was once captured and carted off to a bonfire prepared in a field for his departure, from which he managed to escape by the skin of his teeth. The newspapers loved it and reported the juicy bits with relish. Their columns were often occupied with Claydon news after they had announced the arrival of Ignatius in January 1863 as 'Introduction of a monk at Claydon'. The Rector of Coddenham even made some builders remove a brick which Ignatius had blessed whilst walking through his village. It had been placed in position in the wall of a house which was being erected, and the builders had to dismantle part of the wall in order to get it out.

Drury, however, was ready for opposition and he retaliated quite capably. He was fined £5 by the local Magistrates for allegedly striking a drunken parishioner, who had come into the church and would not leave, with a piece of wire used to rake out the church stove. According to the Rector the wire was quite hot and in the scuffle it had touched the man's forehead; and he returned to the pub where people embellished the wound with red paint. To his opponents, however, Drury had definitely struck the man with a 'red-hot poker'. One interesting result of this incident was that Drury was presented with a lectern Bible, inscribed with the testimonial 'Dear Father in Christ' and expressing 'grief and pain about the wicked and unjust sentence pronounced against you'. It was signed by the drunken man's father and mother and about 100 Claydon inhabitants and worshippers at the church.

There was more trouble when Fr Drury opened his convent for Benedictine nuns in the village. About 1867, a furious father brought some labouring men to break into the convent and forcibly remove his daughter who had joined the

Order. Drury braced himself for the attack and the girl ran off and hid upstairs. One man was observed breaking through a kitchen window and Drury heaved a basin of cold water in his face, then the attack was renewed with sledge-hammers at the doors and entry was gained. Two strong men forcibly held Drury and the house was searched and ransacked. The girl was dragged off and was confined as a lunatic for nearly a year. Then her father died and "Sister Theresa" was back.

Drury, for his part, did not mince his words about militant Protestants: he compared the Church Association with the Ancient Order of Assassins and was known to have referred to Protestantism as 'poison'. In 1878 the Bishop sent him a second monition to remove certain illegal ornaments from his church but this appears to have been ignored.

Then came the unfortunate incident in 1878 when Drury, obeying the precepts of Canon Law, refused to read the Burial Service over an unbaptised infant of a Baptist family at Akenham Church and had an altercation with a Dissenting Minister who arrived to conduct a service at the graveside. Drury felt that one of the newspapers had libelled him and he sued the newspaper. Although he won his case he was awarded only 40 shillings. The Akenham Burial Case has been superbly detailed in Ronald Fletcher's book of that name. It was one of several incidents that led to the Burial Laws Amendment Act of 1880.

Over in West Suffolk, in the Diocese of Ely, J. W. H. Molyneux, Vicar of St Gregory and St Peter, Sudbury, had to endure his share of opposition, particularly through the correspondence columns of the newspapers. His ritual practices were mild compared with Drury's, but he taught the Catholic Faith unashamedly from his pulpits. It was said that 'next to Mr Drury' he was 'the most notorious man in the county for his Puseyism'. Bishop Turton of Ely (1845-64) was alleged to have described him as 'the most troublesome clergyman in my Diocese', and Bishop Browne (1864-73) was criticised because he seemed more tolerant towards him. Fr Molyneux enraged Protestants by daring to state that the Holy Communion was the only proper service appointed for Sundays and that the whole congregation should stay for it, including non-communicants. On one occasion in 1866 he preached such a vehement sermon along these lines that it brought about a flood of opposition in the newspapers.

There had been trouble when he had removed the pews at St Peter's Church and sold them on the Market Hill, substituting chairs in the church in order to stamp out the pew-renting system. Sudbury folk were also infuriated when he refused to allow St Peter's bells to be rung to celebrate the marriage of the Prince of Wales in March 1863 because it had taken place during Lent. Despite the fact that the Archbishop of Canterbury had stated that Queen Victoria would quite understand if festivities were postponed until Easter, Sudbury folk were furious and a threat was made to force entry into both churches and to do damage there to windows and furnishings. This did not happen, but the ringers did manage to break into St Peter's tower and the bells were rung.

The occasional legal argument over furnishings took place, one example being the exchange of correspondence between the Bishop of Ely and the Duchess of Montrose regarding the sculpture of the Assumption of St Agnes to be placed in the east wall of her new church at Newmarket. It was some time before permission was granted for its erection and it stood for a time at the side of the chancel covered by a cloth.

During visits to churches, some 19th-century bishops occasionally refused to proceed with services unless offensive ornaments were removed, and clergy and churchwardens dashed around reluctantly to obey their orders in fear and trembling. Suffolk, however, provides a similar tale but with the reverse consequences. Bishop Sheepshanks came to St Andrew, Gorleston (then in Suffolk) in April 1897 to administer confirmation for the churches of the area. Its rather exotic Vicar, the Rev'd Forbes Phillips, who wrote plays and enjoyed a glass of beer in local pubs, had 'tendencies towards High Ritual'. At the commencement of the service the Bishop, when entering the chancel, observed lighted candles upon the altar and desired the Vicar to remove them immediately. Philips refused, taking the view that he had only 'lent' his church for the purposes of

Fr Forbes Phillips.

Confirmation and therefore the Bishop had no right to use the service to object to what it contained. The Bishop called up the churchwardens to put out the candles, but they replied that they had no authority inside the sanctuary rails. The Vicar then told the Bishop to make up his mind about what he was going to do – whether he would proceed with the service or not. He said that he would give him a minute in which to do so and promptly took out his watch. As about 15 minutes had already been taken up by argument, the Bishop waived his objection for the sake of peace, but showed his displeasure by refusing to join the procession at the end of the service.

Fr Forbes Phillips was delighted when the stone mensa slab from the mediæval High Altar, removed at the Reformation, was discovered buried beneath the sanctuary floor in 1906. He had it restored to its rightful place and solemnly rededicated it for its proper use. It remains in place in Gorleston's beautiful (and now Evangelical) parish church, placed on polished marble columns supporting mock Norman arches. A stone tablet hidden beneath it records its history (at least in Fr Phillips' opinion – he thought that it was Norman and that it was cast out by the Puritans) and restoration.

The activities taking place at Kirkley during the late 19th century caused the Rector of the adjacent parish of Pakefield to wage a personal vendetta against the "Popery" there. The Rev'd Lewis Price (Rector of Pakefield 1871-1901) had once been a friend of Henry James Prince and for a while had been part of his notorious "Agapemane" set-up (the Abode of Love) at Spaxton in Somerset. The east window in Pakefield Church is his own memorial to commemorate his '25 years of Protestant Evangelical Ministry' there. Canon Stather Hunt wrote that Price's extreme Protestantism and Puritanism served to make Kirkley more advanced; before he came, both churches had been of the old fashioned 'High Church' tradition. When Fr Williams of Ufford conducted a Mission at Kirkley in 1897 and advocated the practice of Confession, Price wrote vehement letters to the papers about it and actually excommunicated a member of his own congregation for attending a service at Kirkley.

Ipswich seems to have had surprisingly little trouble from agitators during the 19th century. There were letters in the newspapers about Canon Turnock's services at St Mary le Tower and correspondents enjoyed taking pot shots in print at Fr Cobbold of St Bartholomew's, who was also occasionally heckled. He expected persecution, however, and was quite capable of dealing with it. He had little trouble from his Bishop, except that as a result of some agitation in 1898. Dr Sheepshanks asked to see copies of his 'extra services', but having seen them he sanctioned them all, subject to a few minor modifications. The words 'Gate of Hell' were to be altered in the Vespers for the Dead, words in the 6th Station of the Cross needed adjustment and also some alterations were requested in the form of Blessing of Palms. In his parish magazine Fr Cobbold politely proffered his thanks to the "Persecution Co. Ltd" (the Church Association) for so kindly establishing his extra services for him!

In the tiny village of Kettlebaston, trouble was brewing at the turn of the 20th century between the parish priest, Fr W. S. Sellon and Theodore Beckett, the Baptist Minister from nearby Bildeston. Since Fr Sellon's arrival in 1894 his advanced ritualism had irritated dissenters and Mr Beckett had enticed aggrieved parishioners to worship in his Chapel at Bildeston. When one of these people passed away in 1899, Beckett informed Fr Sellon that he intended to conduct the burial service himself in Kettlebaston churchyard. Sellon did nothing to prevent him from so doing, but pinned a notice to the church door forbidding parishioners to attend, but instead to come to the Holy Eucharist at 8.00 am on the morning of the funeral. The congregation of 15 at the Eucharist included Beckett, whose behaviour throughout the service was described as "unseemly". Whilst the people were making their communion a small explosion was heard and the church was filled with 'an abominable stench'. A man bolted from the church but could not be caught; he had produced a small bottle of asafœtida, which had been set light to so that it would explode, giving forth a hideous and choking smell which would make any schoolboy's stink bombs smell like Easter lilies by comparison!

In 1900, Beckett was back – this time with an Anglican ally, the Rev'd R. G. Fillingham, Vicar of Hexton, Herts, and a fiery Protestant agitator. He preached at Beckett's chapel, inciting the congregation there to accompany him to Kettlebaston to protest during the most solemn part of the Communion Service at a future pre-arranged date. On the appointed day, Fillingham, Beckett and about 50 Baptists duly turned up. Fr Sellon had heard of the plan and informed the police. Fillingham began his part of the proceedings by going to the vestry and trying to force a document called a protest on the Rector, who refused it, and the churchwardens escorted him from the vestry. At the consecration, Fillingham yelled out at the top of his voice 'Idolatry! Protestants leave this house of Baal!' whereupon he and his followers left for their own open-air service in the road outside. As a result he was convicted of riotous behaviour and was fined £70 by Hadleigh Magistrates for his trouble. Fr Cobbold could not resist recording this in the magazine of St Bartholomew, Ipswich, with the comment that this represented £10 per word uttered! There was an appeal, but it was dismissed, so Fillingham and Beckett had a meeting in the Co-Operative Hall in Ipswich to protest about JPs and unfair trials and to get support for the Protestant Pioneer League. Mouth-watering descriptions of the service were given by Fillingham, who added that if he had given them the slightest encouragement to do so, the determined and sturdy Suffolk men who were with him would have stripped the Rector of his illegal robes as he came out of the vestry.

The Royal Commission for Ecclesiastical Discipline was set up in 1904 to report upon goings-on at churches that were suspected of illegalities. Sixteen eminent bishops, politicians and lawyers, including the Archbishop of Canterbury, met for 118 sessions to discuss evidence of alleged illegalities in churches throughout the country. They heard evidence from informers who were hired to visit churches which had so-called "illegal practices", make notes and report back. A few churches in northeast Suffolk were therefore blessed with a visit from one John Perkins Mayers, who lived at Bedingham, Norfolk, and was the son of a former Rector of Weston. He had worked with the Church Association, so was no doubt delighted to visit services and note the "crimes". His reports are interesting and details are noted, although their purpose and meaning are occasionally totally misunderstood – and, of course, as most of his visits were on weekdays he did not see the churches at their best! The crimes outlined in most cases involved the vesture of the Priest and server and their preparation at the beginning of the Mass (usually they 'appeared to go through some preliminary service'); also the use of the sign of the Cross, bowing, kissing the altar, the mixed chalice, 'making the cross in the air' at the Absolution and Blessing, the Lavabo, the non-visibility of the manual acts of the priest at the Consecration, the elevation of the Elements and the 'secret devotions', and the Last Gospel, are noted. It was always pointed out that these were not to be found in the Book of Common Prayer but rather they came from the Roman Missal. Altars and their adornments are described. In each case the report was submitted to the offending priest concerned; he was invited to reply if he wished to do so.

St Peter, Kirkley was visited, and also its Daughter Church of St Matthew, where Fr P. D. Hedges took issue in his reply with the accusation that he used the Roman Missal, because he did not even possess a copy.

Mayers was greatly preoccupied with Fr Forbes Phillips of Gorleston, especially that he communicated people wearing his biretta and, what was more, he wore it all the time, except for the Creed, *Sanctus* and Prayer of Consecration. This was at a Sunday 12 noon Choral celebration that followed Matins. The church had been 'full for Morning Prayer' but, the reporter was pleased to note, only 20 to 30 people stayed for Communion.

He visited Shipmeadow for the Dedication Festival Mass and was very concerned that St Bartholomew's Collect was used, because he was 'a Saint not recognised in the Church of England'. What was even worse was that there were about 20 children present. Fr Powell did not bother to reply. Mayers did, however, pay a visit to the redoubtable Fr Wakefield, formerly of Woolverstone but then at Pulham St Mary, Norfolk, and the Commission received from him a very lengthy, reasoned and scholarly reply in defence of each "illegal" act, quoting from the Prayer Book, the Thirty Nine Articles and from many earlier judgements in the courts.

On his visit to a Wednesday Mass at Mendham, Mayers did show his ignorance a little, being convinced that Fr Harris was burning incense 'by some mechanical appliance in one of the candle flames'. This was because he could smell incense in the church and the Priest had to adjust one of the candles during the service. The Commission carefully cross-examined Mayers about this and also got him into a muddle when he had to try every method short of lying to get out of publicly admitting that he had dealings with the Church Association.

The totally devious and underhanded methods used to secure evidence is underlined in the reply of the Rev'd J. Garner of Ellough – a moderate

High Churchman whose tiny worshipping community was visited one Sunday. He was guilty of wearing vestments, burning candles when not required for giving light, taking the Eastward Position and celebrating with less than three communicants present. Finally, 'there was a Cross in the Church'.

Garner pointed out in his reply to the Commission that Mayers took lodgings with his Sexton on the Saturday and enquired if there was to be a Celebration of the Holy Communion on the Sunday. The Rector saw him and said that although he did not usually celebrate on Black Letter Saints Days, he was prepared to celebrate on the Sunday if there were communicants. The Sunday congregation comprised Mayers, a Miss Murrill and the Rector's son, Jack, who was a minor. Despite the fact that there were only two communicants, because they had turned up (particularly Mayers, who had especially desired Communion) the Rector stated that he did not feel justified in withholding Communion from them and he felt that in a tiny parish such as his, discretion about convenient numbers for communion should be left to the Rector. He added that the vestments and the other customs objected to were already in use when he came. He then expressed his deep grief at the action of the person or society employing a paid spy to communicate at this church.

Mayers was in for a treat when he visited the Solemn Procession and Sung Mass at Barsham. The choir entered the church from the west end and took their places in the chancel. Incense was brought and a splendid procession then took place. The Crucifer, Thurifer and Servers wore scarlet cassocks, albs, girdles and amices and the clergy were arrayed in copes. The procession stopped before re-entering the chancel and prayers were said with the double line of choristers facing each other; they then turned eastwards again and resumed their places in the chancel. Fr Coates then robed himself in his chasuble and censed the altar. The Sign of the Cross was made three times before the Gospel and the whole congregation knelt during part of the Creed. Fr Coates preached in an alb and crossed stole and announced a Mass for the Feast of St Lawrence (not in the Prayer Book) and asked for prayers for 'deceased persons'. As the service progressed, Mayers noticed that water was mixed with the wine in the chalice and the Sanctus was sung to a long musical setting. He was concerned that, except when he elevated the elements, the Rector 'bent over the Holy Table', making it impossible to see the manual acts during the Consecration Prayer. Furthermore, there were over 35 children in the congregation.

Fr Allan Coates – a man whose skill with words matched his skill in art and music – gave a long and detailed reply, beginning 'My Lords and Gentlemen', which made clear several important points. Regarding the visibility of the manual acts at the consecration, he stated 'This I deny. They may not have been seen by the informer, but they were visible to almost anyone who chose to peer about at the solemn moment'. Regarding the book that he was using (because he was accused of turning over several pages between the Sanctus and the Prayer of Humble Access) he stated 'I cannot even turn over pages without being accused of interpolating some ceremony'. He had announced a Communion Service the following Wednesday, which was St Lawrence's Day (and not in the Prayer Book Calendar). Of this he retorted 'Why did he not look at the next Table in the book and charge me with omitting to give notice of the Friday as a day of Fasting and Abstinence according to the rubric'. He added, 'This is the kernel of the matter. Omission and neglect – wilful and careless – are nothing; but to add one jot to the written word of the Prayer Book and you are a law-breaker'. He stated that the Bishop sanctioned his use of incense in the procession because it was not used liturgically in the Eucharist.

Later, Bishop Sheepshanks himself was called in to discuss with the Commission the results of their findings and what he had to say indicates the tremendous amount of tolerance that he had for his Anglo-Catholic clergy. He had been Vicar of St Margaret, Anfield, Liverpool – a church that was far from advanced but was considered at the time to be rather 'High' in Liverpool's very Protestant diocese. He stated that he had been in churches where altar cards were used, but these were quite harmless. His clergy knew that he would not interfere with the use of vestments unless they were introduced against the wishes of the parishioners; in fact, they had been introduced at one church where the people welcomed them and the services at that church were habitually crowded. He did not think it necessary to prohibit the mixing of water with the wine in the chalice as he had never received complaints about this and he preferred that it should be done openly. He knew of eight churches in his Diocese that used incense when its use was prohibited in 1899, and he understood that these had all given up its ceremonial use during divine service.

Perhaps the most blatant attacks upon individual churches have come from the Protestant Truth Society. This organisation, which must have done as much as any to gain sympathy for the Catholic Movement, because of the way in which it has hounded Anglo-Catholics and disrupted their services, continues to make its protests, although now, thankfully, these are usually a little more polite.

They held various meetings in Ipswich during the closing years of the 19th century. Fr Cobbold heard of a forthcoming demonstration in 1898 and wrote in his Magazine 'I wonder if St Bartholomew's will be favoured… I don't think I shall put "Dedication Festival and possible Protestant Performance" on our bills'. They held a meeting in February 1899, which, in Fr Cobbold's eyes, was singularly unsuccessful. He writes, 'Mr Kensit did not go down at all – the visit was emphatically a come-down'. It appears that not a single clergyman or Nonconformist Minister lent his support. They returned in 1906 to the Lecture Hall in Tower Street, the Chairman being there at 'great personal expense', the newspaper stated, 'because all Protestant clergy in Ipswich seem dead and buried'. They did, however, get an offer of £50 towards guaranteeing the removal of 'all illegal objects' from St Bartholomew's, where Mr Kensit had found 'an extreme book' – this was *Notes on Ceremonial.* They then vented their fury upon the Rev'd Caesar Caine of All Saints because of a book which they had discovered in his church. Fr Cobbold was delighted at all this and remarked that these people could not get Evangelical clergy to go on their platform to support them anymore than they could find Ritualists to provide a sensation by coming to argue with them. It is interesting that Mr Cambie, the Evangelical Vicar of Felixstowe, publicly condemned their methods.

In 1903 the Kensitites went to Bury St Edmunds where they let forth about the Mildenhall Monastery, but at the close of the meeting there was an attempt to overturn the wagonette on which they stood and the police had to intervene. There was also a disturbance at Mr Kensit's later lecture at the Athenæum, which was chaired by the Rev'd E. G. Falconer of Old Newton. Also in 1903, Kensit's Wickliffe Preachers went to Ufford to inform the parishioners of the errors in their parish church, holding forth in the High Street, whereupon the Rector waited until their meeting was over and then preached his own open-air sermon.

These people held many more protests, rallies and meetings during the 20th century and several "Popish clergy" have been "exposed" by them. They disseminated an amusing piece of propaganda in 1923, when they got wind of the Solemn Imposition of Ashes on Ash Wednesday at St Bartholomew, Ipswich and distributed bills announcing the following:

'Amazing Superstition at St Bartholomew's, Ipswich. Blackening of Faces for the Remission of Sins. The recent practices in this church exposed in a special Lantern Lecture. Rally to this important meeting and give your witness for Gospel Protestantism against Holy Water, Holy Candles and Holy Soot – some of the greatest deposits ever drawn from the Bank of Humbug'.

Of a far more serious nature was the court case in 1926-7 over the furnishings in St Mary's Church, Capel when a faculty was sought by a local farmer to have

28 articles removed from the church. These included the second altar, High Altar candlesticks, Stations of the Cross, thurible, statue of Our Lady which had been placed upon the stand of a former lectern, a board with notices requesting prayers for the departed, sanctuary lamp, various books – including the *Anglican Missal,* the Tabernacle, sacring gong, crucifixes and Confessional stool. These were finally condemned by the Chancellor of the Diocese (F. Keppel North) although the rood beam with its figures (which it was alleged had been put to superstitious use), the angels on the chancel roof, the processional crucifix, the reredos and the altar frontal, were allowed to remain.

The case was heard in Capel Village Hall and the Anglo-Catholic practices at Capel were given a good airing. Fr Robertson and his two churchwardens gave evidence, explaining the purposes of the furnishings and Mr Packard, the petitioner, produced a document signed by 220 parishioners to back him up. Several witnesses tried to show that clouds of incense, non-communicating celebrations of the Eucharist, the abuse of images, etc, were emptying the church. The facts seemed to indicate, however, that the congregations had vastly improved since Fr Robertson's arrival. One witness testified that on visiting the church he heard a 'mumbling voice' and saw a lady making her confession in the chancel. The witness first stated that the priest's hand was on the lady's shoulder, but later withdrew that accusation.

The *Church Times* found Chancellor North's judgement particularly harsh and was pleased to back an appeal to the Court of Arches, which took place before Sir Lewis Dibdin in January 1928, with interesting results. The Judge, in fact, reversed Chancellor North's decision on two points – he declared that the notices requesting prayers for departed people were permissible, also the Confessional stool and the Crucifix above it, saying that this was greatly preferable to the hearing of Confessions in the vestry or in a Confessional Box. The *Church Times* was therefore delighted to announce that this decision had, in fact, declared that kneeling-stools for penitents, with crucifixes nearby, and notices requesting prayers for the departed were now legal in Anglican churches, thanks to the Capel Appeal. The forbidden articles were reverently removed and taken to the Rectory for a time.

In bringing to a close this selective catalogue of animosity and bad feeling, lest anybody should have the mistaken impression that all people who opposed the Catholic Movement treated it with rudeness and unpleasantness, I venture to introduce a Suffolk clergyman whom one would not normally expect to find in a book about Anglo-Catholics. His influence for untold good, however, amidst the ritual controversies of the late 19th century, is a shining example to his fellow

Christians – Catholics and Protestants alike. He is Canon Samuel Garratt – the Evangelical Vicar of St Margaret's Church, Ipswich from 1867 to 1895, and one of the leading champions in Suffolk at that time of the Protestant and anti-ritualistic cause. He believed the Catholic Movement to be very misguided but had also taken the trouble to study it very carefully. He had known John Mason Neale from childhood and had studied at university with him. Even Dr Pusey wrote of him: 'Mr Garratt, whilst maintaining the difference of his own belief, candidly appreciates ours'.

Garratt believed that the Church Association, with its policy of hounding ritualistic clergy, putting them on trial and penalising them, was very wrong and he refused to be a member of it. He maintained that he only sympathised with 'controversy lovingly conducted'. He had the insight to understand that Catholics would never accept the authority of a secular court 'which could imprison, but never bend the will' and the intelligence to realise that the greater the ill-treatment of ritualists, the more fair-minded and decent people would be indignant at their treatment and so this was doing far more harm to the Protestant cause than any number of ritualistic services. It was this thinking, which flowed from his pulpit and his pen, which caused his Bishop to observe after his death that the charity with which he acted meant that 'those who differed from him most were those who admired him most'.

He felt that the Church Association's main mistake was not crediting the ritualists with sincerity. He even voiced his agreement with Dr Pusey about the lack of Christian love on both sides, and added, 'Evangelicals ought never to have used carnal weapons, whether of law or abuse, and daily have we paid for it'.

When, later in his life, the disturbances of services by Mr Kensit's followers came to his notice, he wrote in the strongest terms that such acts were unworthy of any person claiming the right to the label of Protestant or Evangelical and were directly dishonouring to God Himself.

In 1881 he received a long and kindly letter from Dr Pusey, correcting certain remarks in a pamphlet he had produced, entitled *What shall we do? Or True Evangelical Policy*. He reproduced the letter in full in his 'Reminiscences', stating, 'The loving spirit of Dr Pusey's letters makes it a pleasure to transcribe them'. At the end of the letter, Pusey wrote, 'Do not trouble to answer this; only pray for us and the whole Body of Christ'. Garratt did trouble to answer it, saying that whilst he maintained his views of the truth, he found in more and more of his opponents the Love of Christ 'which, in spite of all differences binds us together as a magnet'.

The Reverend Canon Samuel Garratt.

Appendix

Colour Photographs – Ancient & Modern!

THE PHOTOGRAPHS which follow are hardly a complete documentary of every piece of Anglo-Catholic furnishing remaining in Suffolk. They are, for the most part, modern – it is, of course, impossible to photograph that which is no longer present – so the photographs are mostly of those churches whose worship is still Catholic; be that traditional or more liberal. Although, with a few exceptions, the text of the book looks at the Anglo-Catholic movement before the decision to ordain women to the Sacred Priesthood, some of the photographs depict furnishings added several years after 1992. So the tradition lives on…

Alpheton.

Alpheton – High Altar.

Barsham – Church of the Most Holy Trinity.

Barsham – Nave and Chancel.

Barsham – A wonderful mixture of fittings and adornments in the Chapel of St Catherine.

Barsham – The List of Rectors (left) and the highly decorated Aumbry door (right).

Barsham – High Altar and Reredos.

Bury St Edmunds, St John.

Bury St Edmunds, St John – Interior.

Bury St Edmunds, St John – Eucharistic Banner.

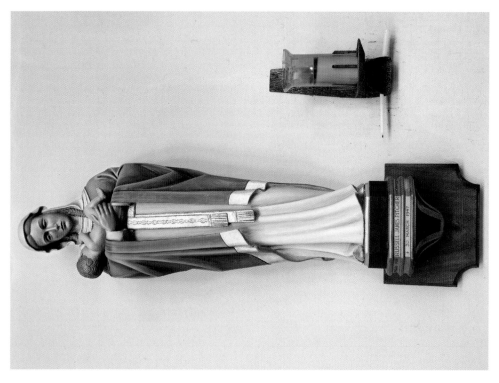

Bury St Edmunds, St John – Statue of Our Lady.

Bury St Edmunds, St John – New Stations of the Cross by Iain McKillop. These Stations of the Cross were dedicated in 2008. They were the result of a national competition, and were developed through interaction with members of the parish and a local school.

Capel St Mary.

Capel St Mary – Stations of the Cross.

Capel St Mary – St Gabriel.

Capel St Mary – Statue of the Sacred Heart.

Capel St Mary – Modern fifteenth Station in glass.

Capel St Mary – The High Altar today.

Cavendish – Detail from Reredos in North Aisle.

Cavendish.

Chevington.

Chevington – Chancel. A taste of France in Suffolk.

Chevington – Triptych on window ledge.

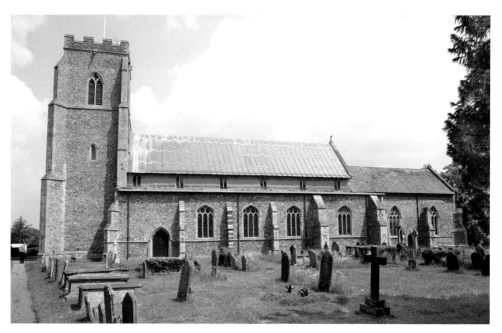

Dennington.

Dennington – The magnificent Interior.

Dennington – Hanging Pyx, lowered from its veiled position beneath the mediæval canopy.

Dennington – Statue of Our Lady.

Eye – The magnificent tower captured in watercolour by Amy Bracey.

Eye – Screen and Chancel.

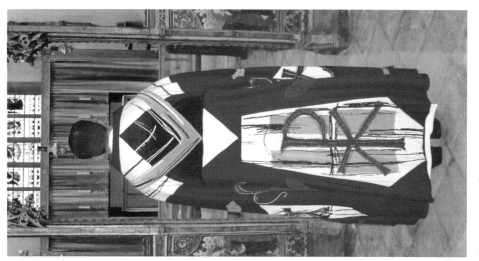

Eye – Late 20th century cope.

Eye – Early 20th century cope.

Eye – The Rev'd Canon Donald Rea.

Eye – Chancel in the late 1950s.

Eye – Chancel today showing the re-ordering carried out in the early 1970s.

Eye – Blessed Sacrament Chapel in the late 1950s.

Eye – Blessed Sacrament Chapel today. Note the modern Sacrament House.

Eye – Comper's East Window.

Eye – A detailed view of the new Holy Water stoup in the west porch.

Eye – Statue of Our Lady, carved by Lough Pendred.

Felixstowe, St John – Interior.

Felixstowe, St John – Lady Chapel and place of Reservation of the Blessed Sacrament.

Felixstowe, St John – Chancel and High Altar.

Felixstowe, St John – Reredos.

Felixstowe, St John – Baptistry.

Hundon.

Hundon – The saintly Fr Waskett.

Ipswich, St Mary Elms.

Ipswich, St Mary Elms – Triptych over South Porch, carved in 2006 by Mr Charles Gurrey of York.

Ipswich, St Mary Elms – Sanctuary.

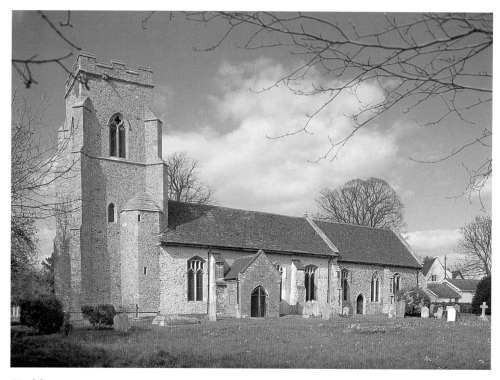

Kettlebaston.

Kettlebaston –
Coronation of Our Lady.

Kettlebaston – Interior in the 1950s.

Kettlebaston – High Altar.

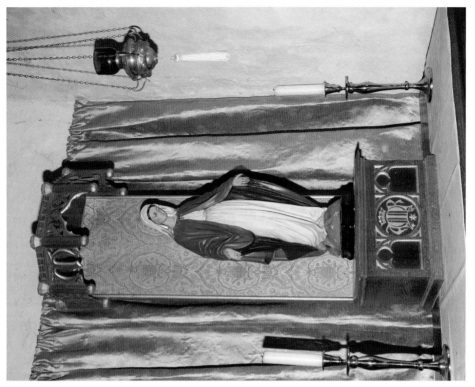

Kettlebaston – Altar of the Sacred Heart (left) and Altar of Our Lady (right).

Kettlebaston – Screen showing St Felix, St Thomas More, St Thomas à Becket.

Kettlebaston – Screen showing St John Fisher, St Alban, St Fursey.

Kirkley – Tower and Baptistry.

Kirkley – Interior.

Kirkley – High Altar.

Kirkley – Baptistry.

Kirkley – Chapel of St Matthew with the Altar from St Matthew's Mission Church.

Kirkley – Lady Chapel.

Lakenheath.

Lakenheath – The reversible Nave Altar.

Lakenheath – The reversible Nave Altar showing its Lenten and Passiontide face.

Lakenheath – Statue of Our Lady, brought here from Eye Parish Church in 1974.

Lakenheath – Font and Paschal Candle.

Mendlesham.

Mendlesham – Blessed Sacrament Chapel. A light burns before the reliquary niche in the Altar.

Mendlesham – Chapel of All Souls located in the south porch.

Mendlesham – Statue of Our Lady of Walsingham in the disused Priest's doorway.

Mendlesham – Lady Chapel.

Mendlesham – Confessional.

Ufford – Nave and Chancel. Note the famous Pre-Reformation font cover.

Ufford – Statue of Our Lady.

Ufford – Eikon of Our Lady and Our Lord.

Ufford – High Altar vested with a magnificent frontal.

Ufford – Side altar reredos by Sir Ninian Comper.